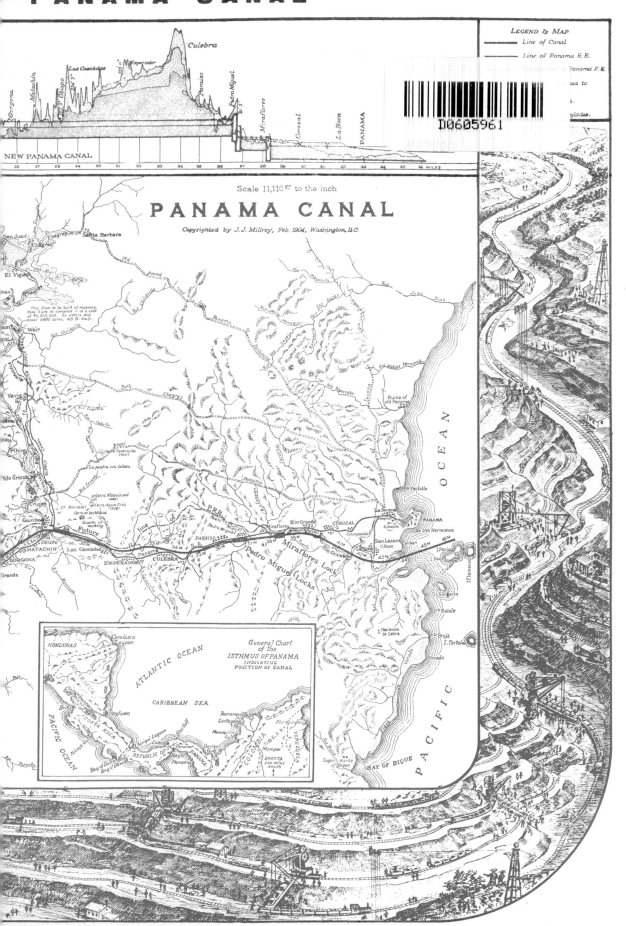

Scale 11,110 ᵗᵗ to the inch

PANAMA CANAL

Copyrighted by J.J. Millroy, Feb. 1904, Washington, D.C.

The Controversy Over a New Canal Treaty Between the United States and Panama

A Selective Annotated Bibliography
of United States, Panamanian,
Colombian, French, and
International Organization Sources

Compiled by Wayne D. Bray
under the direction and supervision of
the Hispanic Law Division, Law Library

LIBRARY OF CONGRESS   WASHINGTON   1976

END PAPERS: Map and Workings—Panama Canal, 1904, by J. J. Millroy.

Library of Congress Cataloging in Publication Data

Bray, Wayne D
  The controversy over a new canal treaty between the United States and Panama.

  1. Panama—Foreign relations—United States—Sources—Bibliography. 2. United States—Foreign relations—Panama—Sources—Bibliography. 3. Panama Canal—Bibliography. I. United States. Library of Congress. Hispanic Law Division. II. Title.
Z6465.P3B72   [JX1398] [Z6635]   016.32773'0728
ISBN 0-8444-0213-3   76-608274

For sale by the Superintendent of Documents, U.S. Government Printing Office
Washington, D.C. 20402 - Price $5
Stock Number 030-001-00074-5

Contents

Foreword

In fulfilling its primary task of providing legal reference and research services to the Congress, the Library of Congress Law Library draws upon a collection, numbering more than one and a half million volumes of American, foreign, and international legal materials, unsurpassed by any other law library in the world. Included in this collection are a great many items bearing upon the troublesome subject of treaty relations between the United States and Panama governing the control of the Panama Canal and the Panama Canal Zone. Material on the subject is also scattered throughout many other components of the Library of Congress, reflecting the fact that it is not an easily separable or purely legal topic but one that has been intertwined in the legal, diplomatic, political, legislative, and judicial history of the United States for more than a century, as well as a theme which has been examined or touched upon in varying degrees of depth by a great many authors. Although some pertinent documents are only obtainable outside the Library of Congress (these locations are listed in the appendix to this bibliography), the vast majority of materials on this subject are in the Library of Congress, which has the definitive collection on this subject.

From time to time the Hispanic Law Division, as is true for other divisions of the Law Library, prepares legal reference tools to facilitate reference and research work. Current congressional, academic, and public interest in the subject is sufficient explanation for the production of this particular reference tool. The reason for making it a responsibility of the Hispanic Law Division might not be quite so obvious, but a consideration of the basic nature of the issues involved will point up the logic of the conclusion.

Treaties are a matter of international law for which there is no separate division, as such, within the Law Library. The two countries most involved in the subject, other than the United States—i.e., Panama and Colombia—are countries governed by hispanic law. Disputes over treaties invoke the international law practices and views of the nations concerned. The Hispanic Law Division is the best equipped to ensure that the legal precepts underlying the attitude of Panama and Colombia, as well as those of the United States, are accurately and objectively represented in the selection of material from those nation participants and in the annotations thereon. Furthermore, a substantial amount of the material is in Spanish and the Hispanic Law Division is the only Law Library component with the necessary language competence.

Wayne D. Bray, the compiler of the bibliography, is the author of *The Common Law Zone in Panama; a Case Study in Reception,* a monograph dealing with the early legal history of the Panama Canal Zone, published in 1976 by the Inter American University Press of Puerto Rico. He lived in Panama and worked in the Canal Zone from 1966 to 1969. He holds a B.S. degree in foreign service from Georgetown University and J.D. and LL.M. degrees, the latter with a specialty in international law, from the George Washington University National Law Center, Washington, D.C. Mr. Bray is a member of the District of Columbia bar, American Bar Association, Inter-American Bar Association, American Society of International Law, and American Society of Legal History.

Carleton W. Kenyon
Law Librarian

A Note on the Use of This Bibliography

For the convenience and guidance of different kinds of users, the entries in this bibliography have been separated into three categories in descending order of essentiality (as indicated by the numeral 1, 2, or 3 at the end of each entry).

Category 1 contains material which is considered indispensable to an adequate comprehension of what the controversy is about and to a grasp of the principal lines of argument which have been advanced by major contributors to the debate. Hence, the acquisition of these publications should be given highest priority in assembling a collection on the subject; likewise, they are recommended reading for the person who wants to get to the heart of the matter in a political-diplomatic-jurisprudential sense.

Category 2 contains material which is strongly supportive or expansive but falls short of being indispensable. Certain entries in this category may be almost as basic as some in category one, but they have been placed here because they present almost identical concepts; recommended reading for the person who wants to broaden his knowledge.

Category 3 contains material which is relevant in a marginal or peripheral sense. That is to say, these publications enrich and deepen the reader's understanding of the legal controversy by filling in the historical and sociological background and illuminating the milieu within which it arose, or by reaching out to embrace material which was more or less vital when written but is now largely outdated.

Publications which are drawn from primary sources are so indicated if that fact is not necessarily obvious from the nature of the material. Publications which are in a foreign language, although that fact will generally be evident from the title, also are so indicated. If the serial set number of a federal document is identified, it is printed next to the call number or location symbol.

Finally, it should be emphasized that the subject of this bibliography, as its title denotes, is controversial—and the existence of the controversy is, in fact, its very reason for being—but the selection process was completely neutral. The sole criterion for inclusion of a given work, regardless of the bias, if any, of the work itself, is whether or not it makes a substantial contribution to an understanding of the elements involved in the controversy.

Rubens Medina, Chief
Hispanic Law Division

Preface

Fixing the boundary of this bibliography at a point sufficiently inclusive to satisfy all reasonably foreseeable needs, yet not so far out and undiscriminating as to dismay prospective users by its sheer bulk, has not been easy. The Isthmus of Panama and its potential as a route for interoceanic communication has fascinated writers, dreamers, and rulers since the discovery of the "South Sea" by Balboa in 1513 and given rise to innumerable plans, schemes, projects, and negotiations. Since the building of a railroad in the mid-nineteenth century, followed by a canal in the early twentieth, leading to international complications engendered by the tangled dealings of the entrepreneurs with the territorial sovereigns, the application of words to paper on this topic has increased almost geometrically. Consequently, there is an enormous accumulation of written records on the general subject.

The purpose of this bibliography is limited to the examination of a specific issue in international law, viz., the treaty relationship between the United States and Panama governing control of the Panama Canal and the Panama Canal Zone. The treaty in force, with some modifications over the years, is the so-called Hay-Bunau Varilla Treaty of 1903, which grants the United States the power to act as "if it were the sovereign" in the entire Canal Zone. The president of the United States has agreed to an abrogation of the 1903 treaty and its replacement by a new treaty in which the right to exercise sovereign powers in the present territory of the zone would be relinquished and control of the canal itself would be gradually turned over to Panama. Since 1965 U.S. and Panamanian negotiators have been working intermittently on the draft of such a new treaty.

While progress has been made, there are still areas of disagreement. Moreover, on March 4, 1975, thirty-seven senators, three more than the number necessary to block ratification of a treaty, signed S.R. 97, which expresses the sentiment of the Senate that the United States not surrender its "sovereign rights and jurisdiction" over the canal. Thus, in both countries, the controversy is not only international—between the United States and Panama—but domestic. While there is strong opposition in the Congress and in sections of the American public to the commitments which the executive has already made, there are also elements in Panama demanding a harder line from their own government than it has so far taken.

The difficulty with any bibliography limited to a specific legal issue is that, no matter how high the level of abstraction on which the issue is argued, the issue has its origin in a concrete factual situation with which it is inextricably entangled. The factual situation in this case is extraordinarily complex and has exceedingly long roots extending in many directions. In order to flesh out the bare bones of the legal issue and give it meaning, the subject has been construed rather broadly. Even so, it was required that a given work pass a reasonably high relevancy test, thus excluding works which are clearly concerned only with, for example, the engineering, toll, sanitary, navigational, or military facets of the canal (except insofar as they are directly and materially affected by specific treaty provisions), and even excluding treaty matters which have no bearing on the evolution or current status of the controversy.

Entries are listed under the following headings according to genus: (I) histories, biographies, monographs, pamphlets, and "travel" books; (II) published official documents; (III) legal treatises; (IV) manuscript collections; and (V) sundry nonlegal periodicals. The appendix lists miscellaneous material outside of the Library of Congress. Whenever feasible the entries are listed in alphabetical order by author or title. Otherwise, as in II and III, they are listed, both individually and by subdivision, by chronological development of the overall subject matter and events rather than by imprint date.

Although the published official documents (II) are the most authoritative and the legal treatises (III) concentrate most directly on the heart of the matter, the broader spectrum of narrative, descriptive, and miscellaneous works are placed in the first-heading position because they provide the setting or background required to fully understand or intelligently judge the more specialized writings. Also, in addition to performing what might be called a general orientation function, many of the historical works contain chapters or shorter passages directly germane to juridical questions.

The published official documents might be thought of as the documentary skeleton of the bibliography. With the imprimatur of the respective governments, mostly of the United States, upon them, they provide solidity and a measure of certainty as to the positions and actions of the governments, or particular organs thereof, at a given time. Perhaps the most important subgenus under this heading are the several treaties involved, the key one, of course, being the Hay-Bunau Varilla Treaty. Also of special vitality and containing a plethora of information are the committee hearings and reports released as official documents by the Congress of the United States.

The nexus binding all entries, especially in genus III but also in the others to a greater or lesser extent, is treaties: their nature, validity, interpretation, and application. Consequently, the juridical questions examined lie for the most part in the area of international law. Serious questions have indeed been raised in the past in the area of domestic law respecting the constitu-

tionality of measures employed in the formative period of government in the Canal Zone, and the lasting effect of these measures is unquestionably an element in the Panamanian demand for changes in the status quo. Nevertheless, even those questions grew out of the exercise of powers presumably granted in the 1903 treaty, and so they refer back to international law. Considerations of international and domestic law merge in another question which is coming to the fore, viz., the extent to which the House of Representatives must participate in any new treaty arrangement involving the transfer of property to Panama.

The manuscript collections (IV), the use of which must be left to the energy and imagination of the individual researcher, offer their own contribution in the form of authentic glimpses—obtainable in no other way now that the actors have passed from the scene—of history in the raw and in the making. Preliminary drafts, rough notes, personal and quasi-official letters, and the like, help elucidate motivations and intentions which sometimes can only be guessed at in the final document on record.

Material under the periodicals heading (V) is more ephemeral, by and large, than the others, yet enough of lasting value can be found therein to warrant its inclusion in the bibliography.

The compiler is grateful to the staff of the Hispanic Law Division, under whose general supervision this bibliography was prepared, for their steadfast support and confidence in what must have seemed at times a task which would never end. Special thanks are also due to the Law Library staff for their generous help in locating the congressional documentary material and to members of the General Reference and Bibliography Division, without whose expertise and patient assistance in matters of bibliographic style this bibliography would not have been completed before the end of the century. I was also given courteous aid from time to time by other employees of the Library of Congress too numerous to mention individually.

Wayne D. Bray

I. Histories, Biographies, Monographs, Pamphlets, and "Travel" Books

The fact that a work appears in this genre of the bibliography may be taken to mean that it has relevance, but does not connote quality. Entries range from the indispensable, firsthand, if biased, recollections of Bunau Varilla (entries 14, 15, 16) and the scholarly, objective opus of Gerstle Mack (entry 46) at one end of the scale to the almost, but not quite, useless travelogue-type books, of which there was a phenomenal outpouring, at the other end. A comment seems in order respecting the latter. As the canal was nearing completion and going into operation— roughly from 1909 to 1915—it seems that anyone capable of writing a sentence, or even those who were incapable, felt an irresistible impulse to inspect this colossal, romantic project and the surrounding hinterlands and write a book about it. Publishers were not very discriminating. The market for such books must have been insatiable. Some of them have been included here (mostly in category 3), despite their obvious defects, because they do provide, sometimes by their very naiveté, an almost photographic (literally so in many cases) picture of the contemporaneous *ambiente* as well as occasional interesting facts overlooked by the more serious and better informed authors.

1
Abbot, Willis J. Panama and the canal in pictures and prose. London, New York. Published in English and Spanish by Syndicate Pub. Co., 1913. 412 p. illus., front. (fold. map), col. plates.   F1564.A13

This is an oversized, somewhat better than average, travelogue with an admixture of light history, personal observation, and social analysis. While the pictures are better than the prose, the latter is not without value, especially when the author engages in impressionistic reporting and manages to catch the temper of the time and place, perhaps better than a more disciplined historian, as in the following commentary (p. 233):

Indeed the prevalent condition of the Panamanian, so far as observable on the streets, seems to be a chronic case of sulks. Doubtless among his own kind he can be a merry dog, but in the presence of the despised "gringo" his demeanor is one of apathy, or contemptuous indifference. . . . It was true they cleaned up his town, but he was used to the dirt and the fumes of fumigation made him sneeze. Doubtless there was no more yellow fever, but he was immune to that anyway.

In the last chapter (p. 399–412) the author engages in some discussion of the diplomacy and politics of the canal. He takes two positions of sufficient interest to warrant noting: (a) that the United States acted questionably, if not illegally, vis-à-vis Colombia and has, in effect, admitted as much by making an offer of reparations; and (b) that the Canal Zone should be fully cleared and "developed" and have a permanent, settled population. (3)

2
Alfaro, Ricardo J. Medio siglo de relaciones entre Panamá y los Estados Unidos. [A half century of relations between Panama and the United States.] Panama, 1953. 32 p.
     El83.8.P2A56

In Spanish.

Written by a Panamanian legal scholar and former president (1931–32) of Panama on the fiftieth anniversary of the independence of his country, this brief tract serves as a good example of moderate Panamanian opinion with respect to the Hay-Bunau Varilla Treaty and relations with the United States as of 1953. The author

describes relations between the United States
and Panama as "cordial" and expresses the hope
that differences will be resolved in a spirit of
mutual conciliation. He ascribes the differences
basically to continuing Panamanian resentment
against the hard terms of the Hay-Bunau Varilla
Treaty and the feeling that it was imposed on
the helpless new republic by force majeure. He
says that the Treaty of 1936 removed some of
the causes of resentment, but not all. In describ-
ing the sovereignty which Panama retains over
the zone, he uses the unusual word *immanent*,
apparently with the same meaning as the more
common *titular* or *residual*. (2)

3

American Society of International Law. Proceedings of the American Society of International
Law at its seventh annual meeting held at
Washington, D.C., April 24–26, 1913 [general
subject: international use of straits and canals,
with especial reference to the Panama canal].
Washington, D.C., B.S. Adams, Printer, 1913.
377 p.   JX27.A5, v. 7

The primary theme is tolls, and especially the
issues raised by the provision in the Panama
Canal Act granting preferential rates to American coastal shipping, apparently in contravention
of the Hay-Pauncefote Treaty with Great Britain. In several places, however, particularly
pages 93 to 126, the discussion explores the
basic question of sovereignty in the Canal Zone
as affected by the Hay-Bunau Varilla Treaty. (2)

4

Arias, Harmodio, *Pres. Panama.* The Panama
Canal, a study in international law and diplomacy. London, P. S. King, 1911. xiv, 192 p.
maps. (Studies in economics and political science,
no. 25)   Micro 24145 TC
Reprinted in New York by Arno Press
(1970) in its American Imperialism series.

Written while the canal was under construction and the author, a Panamanian, was a
student in residence at the London School of
Economics and Political Science, this is a re-
strained, objective study, but not one of great
depth, with principal emphasis on the thesis that
international law demands the permanent neutralization of the canal. Later in life the author
served as president of Panama. His younger
brother, Arnulfo Arias, was the last constitution-
ally elected president of Panama, overthrown in
1968 by a military coup which brought the
present government to power. (2)

5

Arosemena, Carlos C., *and* Nicanor A. de Obarrio. Datos históricos, acerca de algunos de los
movimientos iniciales de la independencia, rela-

tados por los próceres Carlos C. Arosemena y
Nicanor A. de Obarrio. [Panama], 1937. 31 p.
                                                LAPS
Primary source, in Spanish.

This unusual little booklet is not what a
scholar would call history but rather a fragment
of the raw material of history. It consists of the
recollections, dictated to a stenographer in 1937,
of Carlos C. Arosemena and Nicanor A. de
Obarrio, then the only survivors of what came to
be known as the Junta of Conspirators, who
planned the Panamanian Revolution of 1903. It
does not contain anything of great significance
which has not been incorporated into one or
another finished history but is valuable for
filling in or confirming specific details, for
example, that the separatist movement was
started by José Agustín Arango, at the time an
employee of the Panama Railroad. (2)

6

Arosemena, Pablo. *Pres. Panama.* La secesión de
Panamá y sus causas. *In his* Escritos. v. 2.
Panama, Impr. Nacional, 1930. port. p. 160–
184.   F1566.A86
At head of title: Biblioteca Nacional.

Primary source, in Spanish.

This article, published with his collected writings, is the author's brief history of the secession
of Panama from Colombia and its causes. Pablo
Arosemena was not one of the instigators of the
revolution, but passively and reluctantly went
along with it, placing the blame for it mostly on
Colombia because of that nation's rejection of
the Hay-Herrán Treaty which he avidly favored.
In a tract written in 1903 he had belittled the
sovereignty issue being raised by Colombia
against the treaty, fearing it would cause the loss
of the canal to Nicaragua and the ruination of
the province of Panama. Once Panama was
independent and the canal was built, he altered
his views on the importance of sovereignty. He
served as president of Panama from 1910 to
1912. (2)

7

Arrocha Graell, C. Historia de la independencia
de Panamá, sus antecedentes y sus causas, 1821–
1903. Panama, Star & Herald Co., 1933. 277 p.
                                           F1566.A88
"Bibliografía": p. [279–280].
Another edition published in 1934 by Benedetti Hnos. (Panama, 1934. 289 p. F1566.A88).

In Spanish.

A more or less straightforward history of the
Panamanian independence movement as it appeared to a sympathetic historian from the
vantage point of 1933. The theme of the

interoceanic canal is introduced on page 177 and dominates the rest of the book. The mildly polemical element in this part of the book is directed against not the United States but Colombia. Presents a point of view diametrically opposed to that of Colombia as expressed in such works, for example, as entries 181 and 182. (2)

8

Bakenhus, Reuben E., Harry S. Knapp, *and* Emory R. Johnson. The Panama Canal, comprising its history and construction, and its relation to the Navy, international law and commerce. New York, Wiley, 1915. 257 p. illus., fold. maps, fold. plans, plates.   TC774.B17

"Originally published in the Proceedings of the United States Naval Institute."—pref.

With the interests of naval officers primarily in mind, the authors of this collection of tightly written articles have "endeavored to take the comprehensive view, excluding non-essential details . . ." and yet enable their readers to "thoroughly understand the canal, its history, where and how it was built, what it means to commerce and the navy and where it stands in the council of nations. . . ." For the purpose of this bibliography, the most important section is "The Panama Canal in International Law," p. 157–202. (2)

9

Baxter, Richard R. The law of international waterways, with particular regard to interoceanic canals. Cambridge, Mass., Harvard University Press, 1964. 371 p.   JX4155.B3

Bibliographic footnotes.

Although only a small part of this book refers specifically to the Panama Canal, it is recommended reading in its entirety for lawyers interested in the subject because it offers a global overview and helps avoid the overly parochial approach commonly taken by participants on both sides of the Panama Canal controversy. In the section devoted to the Panama Canal (p. 71–88) the author gives little comfort to those espousing Panama's restrictive interpretation of the Hay-Bunau Varilla Treaty finding, on the contrary, that the treaty puts no effective limitation on the exercise of sovereignty by the United States in the zone. A particularly interesting and unusual point is made (p. 72) that the exercise of sovereign rights by one state in the territory of another, with the latter still retaining sovereignty, has an almost exact precedent in the leasing of naval bases by China to foreign powers only five years before the Hay-Bunau Varilla Treaty. (1)

10

Bennett, Ira E. History of the Panama Canal; its construction and builders. Builders' ed. Washington, Historical Pub. Co., 1915. 543 p. illus., col. front., map, plates, ports.   TC774.B49

Primary source (in part).

A bulky, oversized book, lavishly filled with fascinating and invaluable photographs which almost tell the story of the construction by themselves. This opus, despite a somewhat sprawling and clumsy organizational structure, is one of the germinal classics often quoted and referenced in later works. It is not placed in category 1 in this bibliography only because it does not have very much to do with the treaty controversy, the author having been primarily interested in the construction aspect. It can almost be described as quasi-official in that its writing was personally encouraged and assisted by many highly placed and knowledgeable officials, such as William Howard Taft and Gen. George W. Goethals. Approximately half the contents and more than half the value of the book consist of articles on specific subjects contributed by persons with firsthand knowledge, though some with an ax to grind, as, for example, the article "How the United States Acquired the Right to Dig the Panama Canal" by Theodore Roosevelt. (2)

11

Bishop, Joseph B. The Panama gateway. New York, C. Scribner's Sons, 1913. xvi, 459 p. front., fold. map, plates, ports.   TC774.B68

Primary source (in part).

In one sense this is just another of the innumerable histories of Panama and the canal, from Columbus to the completion of the waterway. It is unique, however, because Bishop was secretary of the Isthmian Canal Commission and hence is often regarded as its unofficial historian. Certainly he was a firsthand observer of the building of the canal and the events surrounding the separation and independence of Panama, his account of which is straightforward, factual, and reliable. (1)

12

Bouvier, Jean. Les deux scandales de Panama. Préf. de Frédéric Pottecher. Iconographie réunie par Roger Jean Ségalat. [Genève, Edito-Service] Distribué par le Cercle du bibliophile [1972] xix, 223 p. illus., plates, ports.   HE537.3.B6 1972

In French.

A recent reexamination by a French historian of the record of France's attempt to build a canal from 1881 to 1904, with almost exclusive concentration on the questionable manipulations of the promoters. The title is somewhat misleading as the whole affar was a congeries of scandals involving widespread corruption in financial, political, and journalistic circles. Contains little new hard information but is written in a lively style from a fresh point of view, the French disaster made all the more poignant by brief glimpses of the American success tempered by an even briefer glimpse of current American problems with Panama. (3)

12a
Bray, Wayne D. The Common Law Zone in Panama; a case study in reception. San Juan, Puerto Rico, Inter American University Press [1977] xxiii, 150 p. illus.   DLC

This is the most recent book in this compilation, coming off the press barely in time to be included. The basic mission of the book was to fill a gap in the historiography of the Panama Canal, mainly for the benefit of lawyers. The author describes the process, known in legal terminology as "reception," whereby the American common law incrementally replaced the Spanish civil law in the Canal Zone. The result is a near-encyclopedic reference work on the topic whose corollary theme is the current canal treaty controversy. The concept is presented that the reception occurred as an indirect consequence of the 1903 treaty, and the resulting juridical situation which exists today provides the basic emotional motivation for Panamanian demands for a change in the treaty relationship.

The book begins and ends with observations on the new treaty controversy. The body of the book covers an immense sweep in time, from the Gothic invasions of Spain to the presidential election of 1976, both of which events, together with numerous and sometimes surprising others in between, are seen in context to have a demonstrable connection with this most unusual and vexing treaty problem.

A great deal of history is provided, some of it drawn from unpublished primary sources, along with some legal analysis, which one need not be a lawyer to follow. (1)

13
Bullard, Arthur. Panama; the canal, the country and the people, by Arthur Bullard (Albert Edwards). Rev. ed. with additional chapters. New York, Macmillan, 1914. xiv, 601 p. illus., front., maps (1 fold.), plates, ports.   F1566.B932

Partly reprinted from various periodicals.
A borderline travelogue with some merit. A somewhat disorderly mixture of personal observation and history, but good reading and informative. Sometimes referred to in later works. (3)

14
Bunau-Varilla, Philippe. The great adventure of Panama: wherein are exposed its relation to the Great War and also the luminous traces of the German conspiracies against France and the United States. Garden City, Doubleday, Page, 1920. xv, 267 p. front. (port.)   TC774.B97

Primary source.

This is a very confusing book written just after World War I. On the one hand it is an unbridled, unbelievably extreme diatribe against Germany, but on the other (which is the reason for its inclusion here) it is a kind of supplement to *Panama; the Creation, Destruction, and Resurrection* (entry 16). Though boastful and unreliable, it cannot be ignored because it does contain some supplementary historical material provided by the protagonist in the drama. A more objective witness could be hoped for, but there is no gainsaying the fact that he was present, as was Dean Acheson in another context, "at the creation" and nobody had a better inside view. (2)

15
———Historia auténtica de la escandalosa negociación del tratado del canal de Panamá; escrita por el propio autor de esa convención, señor Phillippe Bunau Varilla. [Authentic story of the scandalous negotiation of the Panama Canal treaty; written by the very author of that convention, M. Phillippe Bunau Varilla.] Panamá, Imprenta Nacional, 1930. 102 p.
                                    TC774.B943

At head of title: Juan Rivera Reyes—Manuel A. Diaz E.

A translation, with editorial comments, of parts of pt. 3, section 2, of the English edition, London, 1913, of the author's *Panama; the creation, destruction, and resurrection*.

A second edition was published in 1964 by Los Talleres Impresora (Panamá) with a different introduction which explains that the reason for republication is to assist in the national struggle for a new treaty.   TC774.B943 1964

Primary source, in Spanish.

The major content of this book is simply a translation into Spanish of certain chapters and appendixes from *Panama; the Creation, Destruction, and Resurrection* (entry 16). Its significance lies in the undertaking itself and in the introduction, which is entitled "An International Blackmail," wherein the translators explain their motivation for bringing out the abridged translation; viz., that the Bunau-Varilla book was only printed in English and French, and in any case is almost unobtainable in Panama where the citizens need to know its contents in order to understand why "international jurists have declared the 1903 treaty a complete nullity for being in violation of the fundamental principles of International Law." The translators assume that Bunau-Varilla's story in his own unexpurgated words is the strongest possible condemnation of the 1903 treaty. (1)

16
——Panama; the creation, destruction, and resurrection. New York, McBride, Nast, 1914. xx, 568 p. illus., facsims., fold. map, plates (part fold.), ports.   TC774.B942 1914
First published in London by Constable in 1913.

Primary source.

No book could be a more primary source than this one, for Bunau-Varilla was indeed, as he claims and reiterates ad infinitum, the architect of the 1903 treaty which was, in a very real sense, the final triumph of his indefatigable, unscrupulous, and single-minded labor over a period of many years. The book has virtues which derive from its firsthand knowledge, but objectivity is sacrificed. The first person singular constantly dominates the stage and all the other actors, from Pres. Theodore Roosevelt on down. For example, he condescendingly depicts William Nelson Cromwell, who was in fact almost as influential as the author himself in bringing about the final result, as "the lawyer Cromwell" who was out of his depth and really uncomprehending of the situation. In brief, this book is "must" reading, but it must be read with caution. (1)

17
Castillero Reyes, Ernesto de J. La causa inmediata de la emancipación de Panamá; historia de los orígenes, la formación y el rechazo por el Senado colombiano, del Tratado Herran-Hay. v. 1. Panamá, Impr. Nacional, 1933. facsim., plates, ports. (Publicaciones de la Academia panameña de la historia, v. 1)   F1566.C27
"Estudio presentado por su autor a la Academia Panameña de la Historia, en la sesión celebrada el 27 de octubre de 1932, al tomar asiento en dicha corporación como miembro de numero y recibir su diploma de correspondiente de la Academia [de la Historia] de Madrid."
Contents: 1. pte. Antecedentes del Tratado Herran-Hay.—2. pte. Historia diplomática del Tratado Herran-Hay.—3. pte. Documentación.—Bibliografía (p. [179]–181).

In Spanish.

A good, standard, dispassionate, objective history by a Panamanian scholar and jurist, of the origins, drafting, and rejection by the Colombian Senate of the Hay-Herrán Treaty, which the author concludes was "the immediate cause of the emancipation of Panama." This book stops at that point and does not enter into the Hay-Bunau Varilla Treaty and the subsequent controversy with the United States. The book was presented by the author to the Panamanian Academy of History upon the occasion of his appointment as a corresponding member of the Academy of History of Madrid. (2)

18
Chidsey, Donald B. The Panama Canal; an informal history. New York, Crown Publishers [1970] 216 p. illus., map, ports.
Bibliography: p. 205–211.
                              F1569.C2C48 1970

Suitable reading for junior high school students. (3)

19
Dean, Arthur H. The Panama Canal. *In his* William Nelson Cromwell, 1854–1948; an American pioneer in corporation, comparative, and international law. [New York? 1957] p. 120–153.
                              KF373.C69D4

Chapter 7 of this adulatory biography of Cromwell gives an essentially accurate, if somewhat idealized by omission, account of Cromwell's activities in the "Panama project" to which he "devoted almost 8 years of his life." Anything on that subject by a responsible biographer (which Mr. Dean is) is important. Although true, this biography does not present the whole truth. There is never a hint that Mr. Cromwell would ever do anything the least bit devious nor that he was motivated by anything other than altruism. To take a random example of understatement by omission, consider the following sentence (p. 104): "He had also worked closely with the Colombian representatives in Washington." In fact, he sometimes wrote the official dispatches from the Colombian representatives to their own government in Bogotá. When the ill-fated Hay-Herrán Treaty, in which Cromwell's client had a vested interest amounting to millions of dollars, was signed at Hay's residence, the only person present besides Hay and Herrán was Cromwell. (1)

20
Dennis, Alfred L. P. The canal treaties. *In his* Adventures in American diplomacy, 1896–1906 (from unpublished documents). New York, E. P. Dutton [1928] p. 156–169.   JX1415.D4

This book concentrates on a brief period of American diplomatic history which embraces the crucial negotiations resulting in the creation of the Canal Zone and the beginning of construction of the Panama Canal. Partly for that reason, it offers more thorough and useful coverage than is found in the more recent but more general diplomatic histories by Samuel Flagg

Bemis and Thomas A. Bailey. Dennis's excerpt deals with the Hay-Pauncefote treaties.

Though not part of the chapter cited in this entry, an earlier passage from the book (p. 12) is worth quoting because it throws light on the author's perspective and represents a view still shared by many Americans:

It appears that President Roosevelt exceeded his authority at the time of the revolution in Panama. Others who differ with me are, however, united with me in supporting the view that Panama was justified in rebellion. As a result, the Republic of Panama was restored to its independent condition and promptly gave to the United States the right to the Canal Zone. Later the United States wisely recognized the interest of Colombia and generously paid to her $25,000,000. From the point of view of economic and political interest, the American policy of maintaining a dominant interest as to the canal seems to me justified for the Panama Canal policy is first of all a policy of national defense. (1)

21
——The Panama Canal. *In his* Adventures in American diplomacy, 1896–1906 (from unpublished documents). New York, E.P. Dutton [1928] p. 309–345.   JX1415.D4

This entry should be read immediately after entry 20. The general remarks about the book therein apply equally to this entry, which deals with the circumstances surrounding the Hay-Herrán and the Hay-Bunau Varilla treaties. It ends on this somewhat complacent note (p. 336):

The title of the United States is now clear and an American Canal, built by the United States, protected by her army and navy, today stands as the achievement of American engineers and scientists. The power, the eagerness, and the vigilance of President Roosevelt stand evident. (1)

22
Dubois, Jules. Danger over Panama. Indianapolis, Bobbs-Merrill [1964] 409 p.   F1567.D8
     Bibliography: p. 399–401.

Published shortly after the riots of January 1964, which apparently inspired, in part, the writing of the book and to which a good deal of space is given. Emphasis is on external threats to, and intervention in, Panama and the Canal Zone, first by Nazi Germany and Japan, then in the postwar era by Castro and international communism; but the relevance of these matters to the U.S.-Panamanian controversy over the canal is also demonstrated. Contains some fascinating bits of miscellaneous, but in varying degrees relevant, information not often, if ever, found in other books; for example, the activities of Thelma King (see entry 39), pro-Communist lawyer and former deputy, during the 1964 riots. Another example is the author's allegation that Alger Hiss (p. 315–16) deliberately precipitated a conflict with Panama in the United

Nations over non-self-governing territories (see entry 187), a charge previously made by Earl Harding (see entry 34).

While some may consider the book overly alarmist and sensational, it appears to be responsibly documented, and the author is obviously knowledgeable, having lived in Panama and the zone and attended law school at the University of Panama. (2)

23
Du Val, Miles P. And the mountains will move, the story of the building of the Panama Canal. Stanford University, Calif., Stanford University Press; London, G. Cumberlege, Oxford University Press [1947] xvi, 374 p. facsim., maps (1 fold.), plates, ports. (The Du Val Panama Canal series [v. 2])   HE537.8.D86
     Stanford books in world politics.
     "References consulted": p. 348–360.

This book is a companion and, to a certain extent, a sequel to *Cadiz to Cathay* (entry 24) by the same author. It has become a much quoted classic account of the construction period, including the construction of the Panama Railroad and the unsuccessful French effort to build a canal. The author feels other books have not given the French credit commensurate to their actual accomplishments during this period. While there is not a great deal of factual material which has not already been published, the book is well organized for easy assimilation, is beautifully written, and has a flavor of authenticity which is perhaps partly explained by the fact that the author was captain of the port of the Pacific Terminal of the Canal from 1941 to 1944. (2)

24
——Cadiz to Cathay; the story of the long diplomatic struggle for the Panama Canal. New York, Greenwood Press, 1968 [1947] xix, 548 p. illus., facsims., maps, ports.
     HE537.8.D87 1968
     Includes bibliographies.
     First published in 1940.

This is one of the classic histories of "the long diplomatic struggle," a product of sound scholarship drawing in large part upon primary sources such as manuscript collections and actual interviews with then still living participants in the events. The author, as a result of convictions acquired from his research of source materials, stresses one point in particular which he feels has not been given sufficient recognition by other authors; viz., the role of Senator Morgan of Alabama in keeping the canal project alive during the many discouraging years preceding fruition. Though Morgan fought to the last for the Nicaraguan route, he accepted the fait accompli of the Spooner Act and thereafter became the leading Senate spokesman for complete "Americanization" of the Canal Zone.

The book is better history than prophecy. The author considered the Hay-Bunau Varilla Treaty a considerable improvement over the ill-fated Hay-Herrán Treaty because it created "a Canal Zone government separate from the Panama government" and thus "permanently removed, what probably would have been a perpetual cause of conflict and recrimination . . ." which would have resulted from a "duality of control." He goes on to say that the 1903 treaty "resulted in extensive public recrimination," but concludes that ". . . before long the scars of the controversy will disappear, the wounds will be forgotten . . . ." Of course, that was written in 1940 and was an optimistic view which was then generally shared by those few Americans who gave any thought at all to the matter but not as generally accepted by Panamanians who thought about it. (1)

25
Du Val, Miles P., *and* Almon R. Wright. Panama Canal. *In* Encyclopaedia Britannica. v. 17. Chicago, Encyclopaedia Britannica [1973] p. 205–213.　　　　　　　　　　AE5.E363 1973

Divided into three main parts—The Waterway, The Canal Zone, and History—this tightly written article packs a remarkable amount of information into a small space. Factually reliable, it is recommended for the reader who wants to absorb the optimum amount of basic data in the least possible time. (2)

26
Ealy, Lawrence O. Yanqui politics and the Isthmian Canal. University Park, Pennsylvania State University Press [1971] 192 p.
　　　　　　　　　　　　　E183.8.P2E15

"A Rider College publication."

Bibliography; p. [178]–185.

Quoting from the preface:

During the course of several years of research into the history of Panama and of writing about the isthmus and the canal, I have been intrigued by the frequency with which the subject of an interoceanic canal became a matter of political action and controversy in the United States. . . . The main purpose of this book is to provide a comprehensive chronology of the political issues surrounding the Panama Canal without, however, delving into tedious detail of interest only to the most dedicated and specialized scholars.

Though going over much of the same ground that has been treaded many times before, the author has succeeded in the difficult task of imparting a touch of freshness and originality to his defined subject. Admirably organized, thought-provoking, and objective. Chapter 9,

"The Yanqui Legal System in the Canal Zone," is an adaptation of an earlier legal treatise by the same author (entry 213). Ealy is probably the first writer to attempt a serious study of the clash between legal systems brought about by the introduction of Anglo-American common law into the Canal Zone. (1)

27
Foster, John W. The Monroe Doctrine. *In his* A century of American diplomacy; being a brief review of the foreign relations of the United States, 1776–1876. Boston, Houghton, Mifflin, 1901. p. 438–478.　　　JX1407.F7 1901

The relevance of the Monroe Doctrine to a possible future canal connecting the Atlantic and Pacific oceans first came to public attention in 1825 with the assembling by Simón Bolívar of what was known as the Panama Congress. The United States was invited to attend, but Congress was so dilatory about it that by the time the U.S. representatives arrived the Panama Congress was over. Nevertheless, the action was symbolic and thereafter the Monroe Doctrine was never out of the minds of European powers contemplating building a canal.

The author discusses the Clayton-Bulwer Treaty which he calls (p. 457) ". . . the most serious mistake in our diplomatic history, and . . . the single instance, since its announcement in 1823, of a tacit disavowal or disregard of the Monroe Doctrine. . . ." While this is a classic examination of the Monroe Doctrine, it was written before the Hay-Pauncefote Treaty and consequently is of limited relevance to the current treaty controversy with Panama. (2)

28
Fraga Iribarne, Manuel. El Canal de Panamá; geopolítica, diplomacía y derecho internacional. Madrid [Consejo Superior de Investigaciones Científicas, Instituto Francisco de Vitoria, Sección de Derecho Marítimo] 1953. 56 p. illus. (Colección de estudios de derecho internacional marítimo. Serie C: Ensayos, num. 3)　JX1398.F7

In Spanish.

This work is one of a "collection of studies of international maritime law" published under the auspices of the Merchant Marine Ministry of Spain. It is scholarly, historically accurate, and objective, but does not present any novel viewpoints nor contain any information which cannot be found in numerous other works. Therein lies perhaps its chief interest, considering its provenance. Though written by a Spaniard in at least a quasi-official position at a time when U.S. relations with Spain were still suffering from the aftereffects of World War II, it forgoes opportunities to stir the ashes of the Spanish-American

War, draws to a large extent on American sources, and refrains from criticizing the American position in international law vis-à-vis Panama.

It may be of some interest also to note that the author was the first vice-premier for the interior of the post-Franco government and the leader of the reformist element in the cabinet. During the summer of 1976 he resigned in protest when the king reorganized his cabinet. (2)

29
Franck, Harry A. Zone policeman 88; a close range study of the Panama Canal and its workers. New York, The Century Co., 1913. 314 p. illus.   F1569.C2F8 1970
Reprinted in New York by Arno Press (1970) in its American Imperialism series.

Primary source.

Far superior to the average run of travel books so numerous in that time period. The author is a sophisticated world traveler, an American fluent in Spanish (a rarity among authors of the day purporting to tell all about Panama and the zone), who spent a few months in 1912 technically as a zone policeman but actually as a census taker, which took him throughout the zone and into all strata of the population. This work is placed in category 3 because its relevance to the current treaty controversy is rather remote—consisting chiefly in astute observations about racial, social, and economic relationships which are still part of the problem—but it is recommended reading on its own merits for anyone who has the time. Frequently referenced and quoted in later books. (3)

30
Fraser, *Sir* John F. Panama and what it means. London, New York, Cassell, 1913. 291 p. front., maps, plates.   F1564.F84
This book is selected as being fairly representative of the many travelogues. Its value lies in adding another shade of local color for those interested in sampling the whole spectrum.

At the beginning (p. 2), Fraser makes the usual reference to diplomatic and political factors:

Exactly how the Americans got from the Republic of Panama complete control of a stretch of country ten miles wide, and reaching forty miles from the Atlantic to the Pacific, and the agency whereby the Republic of Panama came into being at all—declaring independence from the Republic of Colombia which was a necessary preliminary to the deal between the Americans and the Panamanians—is a complicated story with different versions.

Later on in the book he offers his version, which adds little and is not accurate; for exam-

ple (p. 163), he says the Hay-Herrán Treaty provided for a zone "just over three miles wide" whereas in fact it was 6.21 miles wide. (3)

31
Freehoff, Joseph C. America and the canal title; or, An examination, sifting and interpretation of the data bearing on the wresting of the Province of Panama from the Republic of Colombia by the Roosevelt administration in 1903 in order to secure title to the Canal Zone. New York [1916] 404 p.   F1566.F85

This book is a heated, but well reasoned and documented indictment of the actions of the U.S. government, and particularly of Pres. Theodore Roosevelt himself, in connection with the Panamanian secession from Colombia which, of course, was an essential condition precedent to the Hay-Bunau Varilla Treaty on which the legitimacy of the Canal Zone rests. Its factual material is drawn largely from *The Story of Panama* (see entry 111) and *Diplomatic History of the Panama Canal* (see entry 113). Quoting from the preface (p. 6):

The significant facts have been assembled and sifted in our search to determine whether we have a clear title to the Canal Zone. They unmistakably show that it was taken by force. The payments to our partner in crime do not clear the title of its stain. *It is stolen.* Gilding the *political crime* with the gloss of fine words does not remove the *national disgrace.*

The author claims (p. 6) that this "is the first comprehensive account in book form of the events connected with our acquisition of the Canal Zone." It is not clear whether he was aware of the work by Norman Thomson (entry 68), the preface to which is dated January 1, 1915, whereas the preface to this book is dated November 15, 1915. (For Roosevelt's side of the argument, in his own words, see entry 255). (2)

32
Goethals, George W. Government of the Canal Zone. Princeton, Princeton University Press, 1915. 106 p. front., plates. (The Stafford Little Lectures for 1915)   JL1675.G4

Primary source.

This is an amazingly succinct account of both the policies and the machinery by which the Canal Zone was governed during the construction period, that is to say, from the Spooner Act of 1902 to the effective date (April 1, 1914) of the permanent government stipulated in the Panama Canal Act of 1912. Although brief, it does not omit any important fact, event, or issue relating to the subject, nor does it evade the unpleasant truth that some of the things which were done might not have been exactly legal but they were considered necessary to get the canal built.

The author was chairman of the last (third) Isthmian Canal Commission from April 1, 1907, and governed the zone absolutely from January 6, 1908. Though it is mostly a recitation of known facts, nobody was in a better position to know those facts and speak with authority about them. Occasionally Goethals offers us a brief glimpse of his personal attitude and the rationalization for certain actions. Mostly he sticks closely to his subject, which is the internal government of the zone, but now and then (see p. 55 and 61) he ventures briefly into international law; and on p. 85 he says: "It must be remembered that we have, after all is said and done, only a right of way for a canal. . . ." (1)

33

Hammarskjold Forum, 6th, New York, May 28, 1964. The Panama Canal; background papers and proceedings. Richard R. Baxter and Doris Carroll, authors of the working paper. Dobbs Ferry, N. Y., Published for the Association of the Bar of the City of New York by Oceana Publications, 1965. viii, 118 p. maps.

JX1398.H3 1964

Bibliography: p. 96–108.

This is the sixth in a series of books based on the Hammarskjold forums conducted by the Association of the Bar of the City of New York as case studies on the role of law in the settlement of international disputes. Each book is intended to provide, "in brief and readable form, the essential background information on a specific controversy. . . ." The specific controversy with which this volume is concerned is the continuing dispute between the United States and Panama over the Panama Canal and the Canal Zone. Attention is concentrated on the crisis period from the riots of January 1964 to the reestablishment of diplomatic relations on April 3, 1964, pursuant to a formula of accord whereby negotiations were initiated which have continued, with some interruptions, to the present time. The introduction concludes: "The alternative to a just and viable solution can only be continuing conflict, the impact of which will be felt not only in Panama and the other American republics but throughout the world."

This is a hard-hitting, thought-provoking forum which goes directly to the vital questions involved. The participants are: Richard Reeve Baxter (see entry 9), Joseph A. Califano, Jr., Joseph Simpson Farland, former ambassador to Panama, and Victor C. Folsom. The appendix, which comprises approximately half the book, is a reproduction of entry 190. (1)

34

Harding, Earl. The untold story of Panama. New York, Athene Press [1959] 182 p.

E183.8.P2H26

A bit on the sensational side, this book consists of, in good part, an exposé of alleged communist-inspired plots to "give away" or "internationalize" the Panama Canal. Thus, one of the author's purposes is to stiffen resistance to any further weakening of existing U.S. treaty rights in the canal and the zone. He dates the "beginning of Uncle Sam's worldwide giveaways" to the Alfaro-Hull Treaty of 1936.

Mainly, however, this entry is the author's version of the history of the creation of the Republic of Panama, which he justifies by claiming to be in possession of important facts never before divulged. In order to understand how he came into possession of these facts, it is necessary to advert to the famous Panama libel suit of Theodore Roosevelt against the publishers of the *World* (see entry 111, p. 299–311). Of all the *World*'s editors and lawyers who took part in that struggle from 1908 to 1910, the author was the sole survivor at the time of the book's writing, and he claimed to be working from original documents which had been in storage since the litigation. His writing about these documented historical events does have a ring of authenticity and contains some interesting inside information on the machinations of Bunau Varilla and Cromwell.

One of the more intriguing tidbits is the author's attributing (p. 109–110) the 1946 controversy in the United Nations (see entries 187 and 188) over listing the Canal Zone as a "non-self-governing" territory of the United States to a deliberate provocation by Alger Hiss. (2)

35

Haskin, Frederic J. The Panama Canal. Garden City, N. Y., Doubleday, Page, 1913. 386 p. illus., fold. col. front., plates, ports.

TC774.H4

It is indicated in the preface that:

The primary purpose of this book is to tell the layman the story of the Panama Canal. It is written, therefore, in the simplest manner possible, considering the technical character of the great engineering feat itself, and the involved complexities of the diplomatic history attaching to its inception and undertaking.

The stated purpose is achieved, but the result may seem oversimplified to the knowledgeable reader.

The author claims that much of the book was read and corrected by Col. George W. Goethals, chairman and chief engineer of the Isthmian Canal Commission. This seems as good a place as any for the compiler to note that a staggering number of books make the same claim. (3)

36

Howarth, David A. Panama; four hundred years of dreams and cruelty. New York, McGraw-Hill [1966] 297 p. map.

F1566.H6 1966

Bibliography: p. 287–291.

Issued also by Collins (London, 1966. F1566.H59) under the title: *The Golden Isthmus.*

The author is a successful writer of true adventure stories, and in Panama he has found material for another one. There is nothing here of a factual nature that has not been told in earlier books, many of them now out of print; but, as critical commentary for the book says, "the story emerges from David Howarth's pen with a lyric, Homeric strength that is a pleasure to read." Suitable for the reader who only has a superficial interest in the subject and would like to acquire a broad overview without too much effort. (3)

37
Hoyt, Edwin C. National policy and international law; case studies from American canal policy. Denver, University of Denver [1967?] 80 p. (Social Science Foundation and Graduate School of International Studies, University of Denver. Monograph series in world affairs, v. 4, no. 1)   HX1398.H6
Bibliography: p. 63–80.

This is a scholarly study of the impact of international law upon the behavior of the United States with regard to a canal across the Central American isthmus; beginning with the Clayton-Bulwer Treaty and stopping just short of the beginning of the current negotiations with Panama over a new treaty. The distinctive features of this article which make it worth reading are: (a) the distinctions drawn between international law as a decision-making factor and as a legal justification after the fact, and between international law as a decision-making factor in the international arena and as ammunition in domestic political argument; and (b) pertinent biographical material, drawn from unpublished papers, on some of the principal actors in the drama seldom or never found in the standard and more familiar works. (See also entry 217 by the same author.) (2)

38
Johnson, Willis F. Four centuries of the Panama Canal. London, New York. Cassell, 1907. xxi, 461 p. illus., front., maps, plates, ports.
TC774.J7 1907

Quoting from the preface, it is the author's objective: "to show how, by virtue of a somewhat devious train of incidents and circumstances leading from Christopher Columbus to Theodore Roosevelt, this country, in opportunity and privilege, in authority and responsibility, has become at Panama the 'heir of all the ages.'"

Despite its title, very little space is given to the first three centuries. This is a good, detailed history, however, of the subject from the beginning of the nineteenth century to the actual start of construction of the canal. Being one of the earliest general histories, much of it derived by the author from sources with firsthand knowledge, it has been mined mercilessly by countless other authors of more recent vintage.

It is frankly partisan in tenor, finding no fault with anything done at any time by the U.S. government as a matter of policy (though critical of the individual behavior of some Americans). For the concerned reader with limited time (it is a long book), attention is directed to: (a) a cogent defense of the zone concept which shows how the lack of such a zone contributed significantly to the French failure (p. 100–103), and (b) a novel slant on the Treaty of 1846 (p. 170). (1)

39
King, Thelma H. El problema de la soberanía en las relaciones entre Panama y los Estados de América. [Panamá] Ministerio de Educación, 1961. 274 p.   JX1398.K5
"Anexos" (p. [163]–274) include text of treaties and legislation.
Includes bibliography.

In Spanish.

The theme of this book is, quite simply, that since sovereignty is an indispensable attribute of statehood and the Canal Zone inflicts a mortal wound on Panamanian sovereignty, therefore Panama will not truly be a sovereign state until the zone is eliminated. The author is a militantly anti-American, often procommunist (though she has denied being a party member), lawyer and former member of the National Assembly from Colón. Though impassioned and making no pretense of objectivity, this work cannot be dismissed as merely a polemic, nor can its influence on Panamanian opinion be ignored (it was published by the Ministry of Education). Viewed strictly as a legal brief, it makes a respectable case, buttressed by apt quotations from American sources of stature such as Elihu Root, former secretary of state, and L. H. Woolsey, former president of the American Society of International Law. (2)

40
Klette, Immanuel J. From Atlantic to Pacific; a new interocean canal. New York, Published for the Council on Foreign Relations by Harper and Row [1967] 143 p. maps. (Policy book)
TC773.K6
Includes bibliographic references.

After a very sketchy history and description of the canal in being, the rest of this short book is devoted to an almost equally sketchy discussion of the factors and problems which would be involved in a future sea-level canal. The virtues of the book are brevity, simplicity, accuracy, and objectivity. It may serve a purpose for those who favor treatment in a nutshell of a complicated subject. (2)

41
Lee, William S. The strength to move a mountain. New York, Putnam [1958] 318 p. illus.
HE537.8.L4
Includes bibliography.

Another generalized competent history of the Panama Canal and the canal-building period on the isthmus. It would be hard to find much in it that is not also in several other books which draw substantially from the same sources, but that is not necessarily a criticism. (2)

42
Lemaitre Román, Eduardo. Panamá y su separación de Colombia. Prólogo por Abelardo Forero Benavides. Bogotá [Editorial Kelly] 1971. xxi, 706 p. (Biblioteca Banco Popular)   F1566.5.L4
In Spanish.

New, scholarly, thoroughly researched, and written by a Colombian historian from the Colombian point of view, this is the best, if not the only, complete history of the Panamanian separation from Colombia, the Panama Canal, and the relationship of the United States to both countries. Absolutely essential to a well-rounded grasp of the whole subject. The only previous book which can be compared to it (entry 71), though a primary source and hence superior in some respects, is narrower in scope. It is interesting that the author ultimately traces the loss of Panama to clause 35 of the Treaty of 1846 (entry 147) which, as he says (p. 60), was interpreted by the United States at a critical moment in history to have an effect directly contrary to that intended by Colombia. (1)

43
Liss, Sheldon B. The canal; aspects of United States-Panamanian relations. Notre Dame [Ind.] University of Notre Dame Press [1967] 310 p. maps.   E183.8.P2L5
Bibliography: p. 225–232. Bibliographic footnotes. Includes excerpts from treaties between the United States and Panama, the United States and Colombia, and Colombia and Panama.

This book starts out very much like many other histories of the canal but quickly becomes an atypical mix bringing in not only Panamanian bilateral relations with the United States but such varied, though related, subjects as Panama in the cold war, communism, Fidel Castro, the policies of presidents Kennedy and Johnson, and recent (up to 1967) problems concerning treaty negotiations. The author is not strident

but does not hesitate to take positions, such as openly declaring that the 1903 treaty must be replaced with something more modern and equitable.

To get the most benefit from this book it should be read right after Mellander's *The United States in Panamanian Politics* (entry 47) which does for the formative years, but in more detail, what this book does for the later, almost contemporaneous, years.

Some of the author's commentary on Panamanian internal politics became, quite unforeseeably, dated almost before the print was cold due to the overthrow of the traditional oligarchical government in 1968 by the military dictatorship which is still holding power. (1)

44
McCain, William D. The United States and the Republic of Panama. New York, Arno Press, 1970 [1937] xv, 278 p. map. (American imperialism)   E183.8.P2M2 1970
Bibliography: p. 255–267.
Reprint of 1937 edition.

After an extremely condensed, but superbly documented, account of "Four Tumultuous Centuries" in chapter 1, this book is essentially a brief history of Panama, with emphasis on its relations with the United States from 1904 to 1937. It is a scholarly work with no faults worth mentioning except that, for the special purposes of this bibliography, it does not contain much material relating, except by inference, to the origins or development of current treaty controversy issues. Passing from origins to later years, it is not much help either as, for example, when the author says (p. 62): "One of the foremost causes of dissension and agitation on the Isthmus has been the intervention and potential intervention of the United States in the affairs of the Republic of Panama for the preservation of public order." This was perfectly true as of 1937 but the causes of dissension and agitation today are quite different.

The book is particularly recommended for anyone doing historical research because of its excellent footnotes and bibliography. (2)

45
McIntee, Patrick G. An historical reappraisal of the Hay-Herrán Treaty. Washington, 1950. 165 p.   F1566.M26
Thesis (M.A.)—Georgetown University.

Carelessly edited, with several misspellings and erroneous citations, this work is nevertheless of some value, principally because of the wealth of source references and use of the *Herrán Papers* in the Georgetown University Archives, to readers interested in a detailed study of the reasons for the failure of the Hay-Herrán Treaty. It has been largely superseded by the much more scholarly *Panamá y Su Separación de Colombia* (entry 42). The latter volume, however, has not been published in English. (3)

46
Mack, Gerstle. The land divided; a history of the Panama Canal and other Isthmian Canal projects. New York, Octagon Books, 1974 [1944] xv, 650, xxiv p. illus.   TC773.M25 1974
Reprint of the edition published by Knopf, New York.
Bibliography: p. 598–650.

This is the most complete and thoroughly researched general book on the Panama Canal, covering the time span from Columbus to World War II. If a reader had to select only one book for the assimilation of background knowledge, this would be it. Chapters 34 through 41 are the most pertinent to the subject of this bibliography. Though the author has woven, as he says, "into one general history covering the entire field in considerable detail" a variety of elements, he makes no pretense of having any expertise in the law (he is primarily an art historian) and so has wisely refrained from entering very deeply into legal issues. The bibliography is first class. (1)

47
Mellander, G. A. The United States in Panamanian politics, the intriguing formative years. Danville, Ill., Interstate Printers & Publishers [1971] 215 p.   F1566.5.M5
Bibliography: p. 195–207.

The author has set out in this book to write a definitive history of U.S. involvement in internal Panamanian politics from 1903 to 1908, which were, as he says, "the intriguing formative years" during which was established the pattern which has continued in diluted form to the present. The result is a complete success. There is no other book on the subject to compare with it. It draws not only on the author's many years of residence in Panama but on a thorough research of all the primary sources in the libraries and archives of both countries.
The following paragraph from chapter 13, "Conclusion," (p. 189) is a particularly keen and cool-headed summation:

Strangely enough, the United States appears to have been more of a blundering, though not stupid, giant than a calculating strategist. In the beginning she seems to have reacted to events long since consummated rather than to have initiated those projects in which she found herself entwined. Prior to her involvement the Roosevelt administration did not have a particular or definite preference for building a canal on the Isthmus of Panama. Nicaragua would have been as agreeable. Yet by a series of fortuitous circumstances she was drawn to Panama and was alert enough to take advantage of the opportunities offered. But clearly she was neither an imperialist bent upon

aggrandizement nor a ruthless exploiter of financially backward areas. However, as time went by, she was to become increasingly myopic in her desire to see the canal constructed as quickly and as peacefully as possible. This would lead her to adopt a rather forceful policy of paternalistic intervention.

The chief architect of the temporary government of the zone during these years was Charles E. Magoon. For readers interested in more detailed information on Magoon, see *Magoon in Panama,* unpublished master's thesis, the George Washington University, 1960, by the same author. (1)

48
Miller, Hugh G. The Isthmian highway; a review of the problems of the Caribbean. With illustrations and appendixes; foreword by Don Miguel Cruchaga (former Chilean ambassador to the United States and member of the Hague Permanent Court of Arbitration) and introduction by James M. Beck (former solicitor-general of the United States). New York, Macmillan Co., 1929, xiv, 327 p. facsims., plates, ports.
                                    TC774.M62
Reprinted in New York by Arno Press (1970) in its American Imperialism series.

The author is a former special assistant to the attorney general of the United States and holder of an LL.D. degree who became interested in the "Caribbean problem" when he wrote an earlier book about the tolls controversy with Great Britain. (See entry 114 for an explanation of the tolls controversy.) As a history of the Panama Canal, with emphasis on its status in international law, it is not much different from other books of its kind except for a somewhat strained effort to place it in the context of the "Caribbean problem." It hardly acknowledges the existence of any controversy with Panama, but rather takes a world view and high moral tone, as illustrated by the first-page quotation from Elihu Root: "We base our title upon the right of mankind in the Isthmus, treaty or no treaty. . . . it was only because civilization had its rights to passage across the Isthmus and because we made ourselves the mandatory of civilization to assert those rights that we are entitled to be there at all." (2)

49
Miner, Dwight C. The fight for the Panama route; the story of the Spooner Act and the Hay-Herran Treaty. New York, Columbia University Press, 1940. xv, 469 p. maps.

                              TC774.M67 1940a
Issued also as thesis (Ph.D.), Columbia University.
"The Hay-Concha memorandum of April 18, 1902": p. [397]–407; "The Spooner Act": p.

[408]–412; "The Hay-Herran Treaty": p. [413]–426; "The John Bassett Moore memorandum of August, 1903": p. [427]–432; Bibliography: p. [433]–447.

This book offers the most complete exposition extant in any one place of how the canal came to be built in Panama instead of Nicaragua. Though the author modestly admits in the preface that the volume "falls short of being definitive," it remains (though published in 1940) the nearest thing to it and is still quoted as authoritative. The theme and uniqueness of the book lie in the emphasis placed on the author's conviction, also declared in the preface (p. xii):

that the explanation of the secession of Panama is to be found not merely in the plottings of the junta or the prejudicial actions of the United States naval forces on the Isthmus but also, very importantly, in the tragic ineptitude of the Washington and Bogotá authorities in handling the previous canal negotiations.

While the record of ineptitude speaks for itself in the pages of the book the impression left with the reader is well stated by Prof. Allan Nevins of Columbia University in the foreword:

Theodore Roosevelt, a few years after the taking of Panama, complacently said that while the controversy about his course went on, so did the building of the canal. His statement requires a reversal of emphasis. For decades to come, while the use of the canal goes on it will be accompanied by a feeling of moral uneasiness, a sense that the great achievement was clouded by a deplorable and wholly unnecessary blemish.

The more recent work by Lemaitre (entry 42), which also concentrates on this period, is written with more of a Colombian orientation and complements rather than duplicates Miner's book. (1)

50
Otis, Fessenden N. Illustrated history of the Panama Railroad; together with a traveler's guide and business man's hand book for the Panama Railroad and its connections with Europe, the United States, the north and south Atlantic and Pacific coasts, China, Australia, and Japan, by sail and steam. New York, Harper, 1862. [New York, AMS Press, 1971] 273 p. illus., maps.   HE2830.P2O6 1971

Written only six years after the railroad was completed, this is the germinal history of the Panama Railroad, to which all later books directly or indirectly refer. It should be noted that only the first fifty-six pages are, strictly speaking, history, and the rest of the book consists of appendixes of commercial and related geographical data. Makes no mention of relations with Panama, which of course did not exist at the time, and very little of relations with Colombia through whose territory the railroad was built. It is, nevertheless, a book which cannot be

ignored in this bibliography because of the intimacy with which the Panama Railroad has, from the beginning to the present, been associated with the diplomatic, political, and legal history of the Panama Canal. (2)

51
Padelford, Norman J., and Stephen R. Gibbs. Maritime commerce and the future of the Panama Canal. Cambridge, Md., Cornell Maritime Press, 1975. 206 p. illus. (M.I.T. Sea Grant Program. Report no. MITSG 74–28.)
HE537.8.P33

Index no. 74–328–NPT.
Includes bibliographical references and index.

This first-class, recent book is almost entirely concerned with technological and commercial aspects of the canal operation. One section, however (p. 172–85), wherein the authors offer a cogent, dispassionate analysis of the pragmatic alternatives open to this country in the present controversial situation, is highly germane to this bibliography and is recommended reading. An excerpt from the conclusion of the referenced section is worth quoting:

There are limits to how far concessions should be carried. By working to strengthen the effectiveness of Canal operations, while also agreeing to a modernization of the treaty provisions, the United States Government is seeking to forge a new policy that is responsive to international opinion.

Some of the demands made upon it have been made for bargaining purposes. Considerations of national interest must determine how far the nation will go in responding. The nation cannot be expected to sacrifice values that are basic to these interests. It is, however, also in the national interest to maintain cordial relations with Panama.

Norman J. Padelford is also the author of entry 52. (1)

52
Padelford, Norman J. The Panama Canal in peace and war. New York, Macmillan Co., 1942. 327 p. diagrs. (part fold.), fold., maps, tables.
TC774.P14
Bureau of International Research, Harvard University and Radcliffe College.
Bibliographical footnotes.

The author was a professor of international law at the Fletcher School of Law and Diplomacy. The book contains a good deal of general history viewed through the eyes of an international lawyer, chapter 2 (p. 32–81) being the most pertinent to this bibliography. As with most books on the canal written by even the most prescient of authors of thirty or forty years ago, it is generally optimistic in tone and fails to foresee the increasing tension which would develop between the United States and Panama. The last two sentences of the preface, however, though written in 1941, are just as true in 1976, except for the reference to the zone whose future as such is now in question:

No Panama Canal would exist today to pass great ships from ocean to ocean had it not been for vision which saw beyond the limitations of existent realities. The hope for a more ordered future, in which the Panama Canal and Canal Zone may play an important part in increasing the well-being of mankind, lies in similarly transforming present difficulties through enlightened leadership and continued vision. (1)

53
Panama; canal issues and treaty talks. Washington, Center for Strategic Studies, Georgetown University, 1967 89 p. (Georgetown University, Washington, D.C. Center for Strategic Studies. Special report series, no. 3)   JX1398.P33
Reports of a study by a panel convened by the Center for Strategic Studies under the chairmanship of J. S. Farland.
"Minority report": p. [71]–83.

Because of a divergence of opinion, the panel found it necessary to issue both a majority and a minority report. The majority report accepted the joint announcement of President Johnson and the president of Panama on September 24, 1965, agreeing to abrogate the Hay-Bunau Varilla Treaty as a fait accompli and proceeded to examine the alternatives in that light. The minority report refused to accept the view that a presidential statement purporting to abrogate a treaty should be accepted as a definite guideline, urging, on the contrary, the termination of all negotiations to that end and the reassertion of certain rights relinquished to Panama in the treaties of 1936 and 1955.
Now somewhat dated by changes in conditions and the negotiating atmosphere since 1967, this document has unavoidably lost a good deal of its original value; but it is still correct in stating (p. 29) that the issue of sovereignty is the most pressing point of difference between the United States and Panama, while the split between majority and minority reports serves to dramatize the split in domestic public opinion which the commitment by the executive precipitated. (2)

54
Panamá Universidad. *Facultad de Derecho y Ciencias Políticas.* Panamá y los Estados Unidos de América ante el problema del canal. Panamá, 1966. xv, 523 p.   JX1398.P3
A compilation of works published on the subject by Ricardo J. Alfaro, Harmodio Arías M., Gilberto Arías G., Eloy Benedetti, Rubén D. Carles, Jr., Emilio Clare, Ernesto Castillero P., Felipe Juan Escobar, Octavio Fábrega, Narciso Garay, Jorge E. Illueca, Eusebio Morales, Arturo Morgan M., José Domingo de Obaldía, Carlos

Ivan Zuñiga, and the Panamanian Academy of International Law.
"Esta obra representa el esfuerzo conjunto de la Universidad de Panamá y el Ministerio de Educación." [This work represents the combined efforts of the University of Panama and the Ministry of Education.]
Bibliography: p. 507–514.

In Spanish.

This is a compilation of articles on the canal problem from the Panamanian point of view written by leading Panamanian jurists and diplomats over a period of sixty years. It is, in a way, its own substantiation of the first sentence of the introduction, written by the dean of the Faculty of Law and Political Science of the University of Panama: "There can be no doubt that the problems springing from the construction and operation of the Canal on our soil have constituted, from the very beginning of the Republic, the principal preoccupation of every Panamanian."
For the first article, the compilers have elected to republish what was probably the first serious protest by Panama of the way in which the United States was interpreting the Hay-Bunau Varilla Treaty; viz., the letter of the Panamanian minister, José D. de Obaldía, to Secretary of State Hay, of August 11, 1904 (see *Foreign Relations of the United States, 1904,* p. 597–607). In all the argumentation since that date no fundamentally new and different points regarding interpretation of the treaty have been raised. (1)

55
Pepperman, Walter Leon. Who built the Panama Canal? New York, E. P. Dutton [1915] xiv, 419 p. front., 2 maps (1 fold), plates, port.
                                          TC774.P45
The plates are photogravure reproductions of Joseph Pennell's drawings of the canal.

Primary source.

The author of this book was the chief of the office of administration of the second Isthmian Canal Commission, sometimes called the period of the "railroad men," and his aim is to correct what he feels has been the neglect by historians of the contribution of the railroad men to the success of the canal. To quote him directly:

Had it not been for the railroad men (chosen, brought together, and directed by Theodore P. Shonts, who is deserving of credit for their success in the same manner that a general is deserving credit for the victory of his army), the conditions under which the Canal was dug would never have been brought about on the Isthmus of Panama, for it would imply a bolder Congress than has yet met in Washington to finance a third attempt to subjugate the tropics had the railroad men proved unequal to their task after the failure of the Army and Navy regime, following that of the French. It is because no more competent historiographer has arisen for the railroad men that I venture into the breach.

It is a fact, often overlooked as the author says, that Mr. Shonts, a dynamic railroad man who served as chairman from April 1905 to March 1907, built up what might be called the infrastructure—including the work force, the tracks, and rolling stock of the railroad itself—which made it possible for work on the canal to proceed. (3)

56
Rebolledo, Alvaro. El Canal de Panamá; reseña histórico-política de la comunicación inter-oceánica, con especial referencia a la separación de Panamá y a los arreglos entre los Estados Unidos y Colombia [The Panama Canal, brief historical-political review of inter-oceanic communication, with special reference to the separation of Panama and the settlement between the United States and Colombia]. Cali, Colombia, 1957. 266 p. (Biblioteca de la Universidad del Valle, 3)   HE537.R4 1957
Published in 1930 under the title *Reseña Histórico-Política de la Comunicación Inter-oceánica*.
Includes bibliography.
In Spanish.

An excellent, short general history based on careful research, with a clear explanation of the Colombian dilemma in the face of pressures leading to the separation of Panama. Superseded in large part, but not entirely, by entries 65 and 42. (2)

57
Robinson, Tracy. Panama; a personal record of forty-six years, 1861–1907. New York, Panama, Star and Herald Co., 1907. 282 p. front. (port.).   F1563.R65,
        Micro 8983
        F

Primary source.

Despite its title, this book is not so much a personal record as it is a rambling commentary on the passing scene. Tracy Robinson originally went to Colón in 1861 to take a job with the Panama Railroad and simply stayed, becoming the veritable prototype of an American expatriate in the tropics, with the possible exception that he was of a literary bent, even publishing a book of poems at one time. While there is no great depth to this book, it is entertaining nostalgia as Mr. Robinson recalls how the railroad waxed and waned, the French canal builders came and went, and the still-publishing English-language newspaper, of which he was editor for a while, got its start.

Though the book itself made no significant contribution to history, it would probably be no great exaggeration to say that the author did. Toward the end of his long life he had already become a legend in his own time, and no writer on Canal Zone history considered his work complete until he had interviewed the living legend. While the authors sometimes gave Robinson credit, there is no way of telling how much of what may be read in other books are actually the paraphrased recollections of Tracy Robinson. (3)

58
Root, Elihu. The ethics of the Panama question. Address by Elihu Root before the Union League Club of Chicago, February 22, 1904. New York, C. G. Burgoyne, 1904. 36 p.   F1566.R78

This address of Secretary of State Elihu Root, which has become one of the classic statements of the American position in the matter, was delivered while approval of the Hay-Bunau Varilla Treaty was still being debated in the Senate, and in recognition by Root that "there remain good and sincere men and women who have thought our course to be wrong, and many others, whose character and patriotism entitle them to the highest respect, are troubled in spirit." Root says in the beginning: "I am not going to discuss technical rules or precedents or question whether what was done should have been done a little earlier or a little later, but the broad question whether the thing we have done was just and fair."

By and large, that is an accurate characterization of the address, which combines the familiar recitation of the history of the isthmus with an eloquent plea for the inevitability of the actions taken by the United States at the moment ordained by history. Legally, Root seems to rest his case mainly on two points: that Panama already had an established right to independence in international law, and that, in any case, "the sovereignty of Colombia over the Isthmus of Panama was qualified and limited by the right of the other civilized nations of the earth to have the canal constructed across the Isthmus and to have it maintained for their free and unobstructed passage." (1)

59
Saint-Amant, Pierre C. F. de. Guide pour les voyageurs. Route de la Californie à travers l'Isthme de Panama. Extrait du voyage d'exploration en Californie et en Oregon, entrepris, en 1851–52, sur l'ordre du gouvernment français. Paris, L. Maison, 1853. 101 p.
        F1564.S13

In French.

A quaint look at the Isthmus of Panama through the eyes of an imaginative Frenchman in the 1850s. The reason for its inclusion is the way in which it illustrates the fascination the isthmus exerted on many Frenchmen long before de Lesseps attempted to build a French canal, and hence, by extension, the later embodiment in one man, Philippe Bunau-Varilla, of the French dream to see a canal completed.

The book is intended, as its title indicates, as a guide for travelers going to California and Oregon by way of the Isthmus of Panama (at a time when the Panama Railroad was under construction but not finished). It is the author's piquant observations in passing that make the book a delight to read, for example (p. 35), "When Mexico has been annexed by the United States I think that the postal service from San Francisco to New York will be by way of Acapulco, Vera Cruz and New Orleans," and on pages 57 to 58 he informs the reader that the language of the natives of the isthmus is Spanish and gives a brief Spanish-French list of useful words, such as *help, drink, run, mule, be careful, rain, kill,* and *wine.* (3)

60
Sands, William F., *and* Joseph M. Lalley. Pandora in Panama. *In their* Our jungle diplomacy. Chapel Hill, University of North Carolina Press, 1944. p. 1–68.   F1418.S253

Primary source.

In 1904 Mr. Sands was sent to Panama by Secretary Taft to solve the problem created by the constant conflict between the governor of the Canal Zone and the U.S. minister to Panama. Taft's solution was to combine the offices in one man and Sands's mission was to persuade the Panamanians to accept this arrangement despite the obvious inference that Panama was being treated as a mere appendage to the Canal Zone. Sands succeeded, and for a time Charles Magoon became the only person ever to hold both offices simultaneously.

That is the plot of this short piece; but its real value lies in the almost shockingly candid, for a professional diplomat, portrayal of the principal characters involved, both American and Panamanian, and its penetrating, frank, amusing, cynical but not bitter, insight into the realities of the situation. Nobody has ever put one of these realities more succinctly: "Less than eighteen months after the revolution which had created them both, the Republic of Panama and the Canal Zone had become to all visible intents two separate nations. Yet, as in the case of the Siamese twins, neither could draw a breath that was not immediately felt by the other."

Panama's first president, Dr. Amador, usually idealized as a fearless revolutionary, is described as "an elderly and wholly inoffensive little man . . . timid and bewildered" who was put up as a

front in case the revolution should fail. Yet Mr. Sands is not an irresponsible debunker. What he has to say has the ring of truth and authenticity and adds a refreshing leavening to the more orthodox histories and records of the period. (1)

61
Schoff, Wilfred H. Why the Colombian treaty is not justified by facts. [Philadelphia?] 1914. 16 p.
JX1428.C7S3

Defends the position of the United States in recognizing the Republic of Panama, citing the Treaty of 1846, the Agreement of 1861 between the state of Panama and the United States of New Granada, and the Colombian Constitution of 1885.

The treaty referred to in the title of this brief tract is the Thomson-Urrutia Treaty (entry 154) which the author opposes on the grounds that Colombia has no right to any redress or reparations arising from the actions of the United States in Panama in 1903. The legal argument is that Panama was already an independent state in international law because the manner in which Bogotá reasserted its authority over Panama in the Constitution of 1885 was in violation of previous agreements. (2)

62
Sociedad Panameña de Acción Internacional. Panama-United States relations. A situation that must be changed for the welfare of Panama and the honor of the United States. True history of the Panama Canal treaty, born from fraud, perfidy, inequity, dishonor, coercion, chicanery, menace, disloyalty and injustice. Panama's rights on the Canal Zone voiced by distinguished American officials and statesmen. Panamá, Sociedad Panameña de Acción Internacional (Panamanian Society for International Action), 1934. 123 p.   E183.8.P2S63
Micro 22671
E

"Index" on p. [3] of cover.
Contents: Bunau Varilla's perfidy; how the Panamanians were betrayed, by A. V. McGeachy.—The basis of Panama-United States relations, by P. R. Shailer.—The New Deal and United States-Panama relations, by P. R. Shailer.—Our ingratitude to Panama, by P. R. Shailer.—A strange metamorphosis, by J. Rivera Reyes.—Miscellany.—Vices of the Hay-Bunau Varilla Treaty, by J. Rivera Reyes.—Panama's official condemnation of the canal treaty and its treacherous co-author.—A message from the Panamanian people to the people of the U.S. by Panamanian Society for International Action.

Consisting of articles written by Americans sympathetic to the Panamanian cause, which have been based largely on purposively and narrowly selected but undeniable historical facts. This pamphlet is an extreme and impassioned plea for justice, as the Panamanians see it, in the Panama Canal matter. Essential reading as a counterpoise to equally extreme statements of the other side of the case by U.S. Congressman Daniel Flood, Sen. Strom Thurmond, and others. (1)

63
Speller, Jon P. The Panama Canal: heart of America's security. New York, R. Speller [1972] 164 p. illus.   F1569.C2S73
Bibliography: p. 159–161.

The author of this polemic is unalterably opposed to the very idea of a new treaty with Panama. The spirit of the book is captured in the following sentence (p. 70–71): "The Canal Zone is to our people a holy and sacred spot made sacred by the services and sacrifices of those who built the canal and have since maintained and defended it."

A useful and cogent statement of the views and position of the most extreme defenders of the status quo. Contains a short but good bibliography of works which buttress that position. (1)

64
Sullivan and Cromwell, *comp.* Compilation of executive documents and diplomatic correspondence relative to a trans-isthmian canal in Central America. With specific reference to the Treaty of 1846 between the United States and New Granada (U.S. of Colombia) and the "Clayton-Bulwer" Treaty of 1850 between the United States and Great Britain. [New York, Evening Post Job Print. House, 1905] 3 v.   TC773.S94
No. 69 of a "limited edition."
Compiled by Sullivan & Cromwell, general counsel for the New Panama Canal Company.
Vol. 3 includes appendix: Extracts from treaties between the Republic of Nicaragua and other nations.

As explained in the preface, the law firm of Sullivan & Cromwell, as general counsel for the (French) New Panama Canal Company, found it necessary to familiarize itself with the diplomatic correspondence and government documents on the above subject, but could not find a full history anywhere. "It seemed desirable [therefore] to compile this information in a compact form for our own use, and believing that the result of our research might have some permanent historical value, we decided to publish a limited edition of the compilation."

The papers in this enormous compilation cover the time period from 1763 to 1898 and do indeed have permanent historical value. Anyone interested in the current Panama Canal contro-

versy should be aware of the existence of this compilation, even though most of its contents are only marginally relevant to this subject, and those few that are more relevant are available elsewhere in more convenient form.

For a short and readable account of Cromwell's activities directly germane to the adoption of the Panama route, see entry 19. (3)

65
Terán, Oscar. Del Tratado Herrán-Hay al Tratado Hay-Bunau Varilla; historia crítica del atraco yanqui mal llamado en Colombia "La pérdida de Panamá" y en Panamá, "nuestra independencia de Colombia." [From the Hay-Herrán Treaty to the Hay-Bunau Varilla Treaty; a critical history of the yankee highway robbery misnamed in Colombia "the loss of Panama" and in Panama, "our independence from Colombia."] Panamá, Impr. de "Motivos colombianos," 1934–35. 2 v. front., plates, ports. (Obras completas, t. 3 [1ª-2ª pte.])
                                  F1566.5.T47

In Spanish.

Though strongly flavored by the author's personal views, which come through clearly in the subtitle, this is a meticulously researched book which remained the most complete and accurate account of the relations between Panama and Colombia during the period of the Panamanian Revolution until the 1971 appearance of the work by Lemaitre (entry 42). It is still of value and much can be learned from it.

Terán himself was perhaps even more interesting than the book. He was one of the very few leading Isthmians who opposed the revolution in principle because he thought it was morally and legally wrong. He never recanted but remained in the country practicing law and writing this book in his spare time over a period of thirty years. He made no attempt to conceal his animosity toward "Yankee imperialism" (calling Pres. Theodore Roosevelt a "pirate"), yet he practiced law successfully for many years in the courts of the Canal Zone as well as in Panama. (2)

66
Thayer, William R. The first canal treaty. *In his* The life and letters of John Hay. v. 2, Boston, Houghton Mifflin Co. [1915] p. 213–230.
                                  E664.H41T38
Primary source.

Correspondence of Secretary of State John Hay concerning negotiations leading up to the first Hay-Pauncefote Treaty (unperfected) whose object, like that of the successful second treaty, was to abrogate the Clayton-Bulwer Treaty and leave the United States free to build and control an isthmian canal (see last sentence of entry 151). (2)

67

——The republic of Panama. *In his* The life and letters of John Hay. v. 2, Boston, Houghton Mifflin Co. [1915] p. 296–331.   E664.H41T38

Primary source.

Correspondence of Secretary of State John Hay bearing on his role in the secession of Panama and the consummation of the Hay-Bunau Varilla Treaty, interlarded with a good deal of editorializing by the author. Thayer goes to some pains to refute the then current rumors that Hay died partly of remorse for the "crime." So far as Hay is concerned, the two most significant points that Thayer brings out are that: (a) in the last few weeks before the revolution Pres. Theodore Roosevelt took matters more and more into his own hands and made the critical decisions himself, and (b) though Hay did not precipitate or take part in the actual revolution, he approved it and never had any doubts that the U.S. government took the right course.

After he had left office Hay wrote a letter to his successor, Elihu Root, congratulating the latter on his defense of the Panama affair (p. 324): "I have not hitherto spoken to you about that admirable address [see entry 58], I believe, but as a work of art, as a piece of oratory, and history, I think it is incomparable. And, as a legal argument, better lawyers than I think it is without a flaw." (1)

68

Thomson, Norman. Colombia and the United States. A juridical study of another "scrap of paper" and its supersession by the Colombian Indemnity Treaty for the settlement of the Panama question. London [1914?] xxiii, 175 p.
                               JX1428.C7T4

Text of the treaty signed at Bogotá, April 6, 1914: p. xx–xxiii.

This is the most effective argument written by a third party (a Britisher) in support of the Colombian case against the United States in the Panama affair of 1903. By the phrase "scrap of paper" he means the Treaty of 1846 wherein the United States guaranteed the neutrality of the Isthmus of Panama, and he compares the action of the United States in 1903 with that of Germany on violating the neutrality of Belgium in 1914. The first sentence of the introduction is jolting: "Juridically the Panama Canal belongs to Colombia."

By "the Colombian Indemnity Treaty" the author means the Thomson-Urrutia Treaty of 1914 wherein the United States undertook to compensate Colombia for the "wrong" done her eleven years earlier. The author, of course, was unable to foresee the opposition that such a tacit admission would arouse in the United States and that the treaty would not be ratified until 1922 (see entry 154).

Incidentally, lest there be any confusion, the Thomson who represented the United States in the 1914 treaty was not the same person as the author of this book. (2)

69

Tomes, Robert. Panama in 1855. An account of the Panama rail-road, of the cities of Panama and Aspinwall, with sketches of life and character of the Isthmus. New York, Harper, 1855. 240 p. illus., front., map, plates, ports.
                               F1564.T65

Primary source.

The author was one of the first to travel across the isthmus on the Panama Railroad in the year of its opening. It is not the most authoritative history of the railroad (see entry 50), but it is one of the few good firsthand accounts of conditions on the isthmus at that relatively early stage of the American presence, hence often referenced and quoted in later books. In addition to providing general background material, it has some relevance to the history of the treaty controversy in the glimpse provided of how the Panama Railroad operated pretty much as a law unto itself under its own liberal interpretation of the Treaty of 1846. (3)

70

Travis, Ira. D. The history of the Clayton-Bulwer Treaty. [Ann Arbor, For the Association, 1900] 312 p. front., fold. map. (Michigan Political Science Association. Publications, v. 3, no. 8)   JX1398.6.T7
                               H31.M6

Bibliography: p. 309–312.

This book is good history but poor geopolitics and worse divination. Recommended reading only for those who have a special interest in U.S.-British Central American diplomacy in the last half of the nineteenth century and the antecedents of the Hay-Pauncefote Treaty of 1902. The latter was essential to the creation of the canal but is not particularly germane to current treaty negotiations. The author acknowledges in the preface, written in 1899, that, "[s]o intense has been the feeling against [the Clayton-Bulwer Treaty] that its abrogation has often been urged, and is now eagerly demanded by a considerable portion of the American people." Nevertheless, he concludes—just as it was, at long last, about to expire—that the Clayton-

Bulwer Treaty was beneficial to the United States and should be retained. (3)

71
Uribe, Antonio J. Colombia y los Estados Unidos de América. El canal interoceánico. La separación de Panamá. Política internacional económica. La cooperación. Bogotá, Imprenta Nacional, 1931. 442 p.   E183.8.C7U676

An earlier and shorter version of this book was issued in 1926 by Librería Colombiana, Camacho Roldán y Tamayo (Bogotá. 1vi, 115 p. E183.8C7U675).

Primary source, in Spanish.

The author was minister of foreign affairs of Colombia during the crucial period of the Hay-Herrán Treaty and the Panamanian Revolution. As he observes in the prologue (p. viii), nearly all the other principal actors are dead and the story he has to tell is one which he "had a large part in making and wholly lived." Making allowance for the author's natural bias, the book is reasonably objective and sound history. He is not loath to point out (p. xxvii) that he was one of the first to recognize the peril in which Colombia was left by the abrogation of the Clayton-Bulwer Treaty and the results of the Spanish-American War. (2)

72
Verrill, Alpheus Hyatt. Panama, past and present. New York, Dodd, Mead, 1921. 262 p. front., maps (2 fold.), plates.   F1564.V55

This book is dedicated "to my esteemed friend, Doctor Belisario Porras, President of Panama" and indeed the author, who lived in Panama for many years, understands the whole country and its people. The principal reason for including the book is this bibliography is exactly that, unlike most of the travelogue types, it is mostly about the country which the zone bisects, rather than just a once-over-lightly review of the zone and the canal. By widening the horizon a little, it helps to put the zone and the canal in perspective. (3)

73
Wyse, Lucien N. B. Le canal de Panama, l'Isthme américain, explorations; comparaison des tracés étudiés, négociations; état des travaux. Paris, Hachette, 1886. 399 p. illus., 2 fold. maps, plates, ports   TC774.W96

Appendice: Traité de Bogotá de 1846 entre les États-Unis de l'Amérique du Nord et la république de la Nouvelle-Grenade (Etats-Unis de Colombie). Traité Clayton-Bulwer entre les Etats-Unis d'Amérique et la Grande-Bretagne. Contrat Salgar-Wyse pour la concession du canal interocéanique. Lettre d'engagement addressée a Lucien N. B. Wyse par le Comité de direction du chemin de fer de Colon (Aspinwall) à Panama. Echantillons géologiques de l'Isthme colombien.

Primary source (in part), in French.

Lt. Lucien Napoleon Bonaparte Wyse of the French navy surely has a legitimate claim to be called the grandfather of the Panama Canal. Commencement of the canal, eventually finished by the United States of America in 1914, was authorized by the Wyse Concession of 1878 (entry 150). Wyse always felt that he, instead of de Lesseps, should have been in charge of the French enterprise. This is his own story of the great undertaking, from its historical beginnings to 1886, with fascinating maps and woodcuts. He wrote several other works on the general subject, but this is the best. It is quoted several times by Gerstle Mack (entry 46) who was unusually conscientious in seeking the soundest primary sources. (1)

II. Published Official Documents

A. Fundamental Issuances of the Formative Era of Canal Zone Jurisprudence

These three works were published as a trilogy by the Panama Canal Press in 1922. They are well annotated, cross-referenced, and more or less interdependent.

74

U.S. *Treaties, etc.* Treaties and acts of Congress relating to the Panama Canal. Annotated 1921. Mount Hope, C.Z., Panama Canal Press, 1922. 258 p.   TC773.U6 1921a

Contains all the most important treaties preceding the date of issuance with the notable exceptions of the Treaty of 1846 with New Granada and the Hay-Herrán Treaty of 1903 (which was never perfected and hence was not, properly speaking, a treaty). Also contains the most important acts of Congress preceding date of issuance (p. 30, 34, 79) together with all other acts, however trivial. (1)

75

U.S. *President.* Executive orders relating to the Panama Canal (March 8, 1904, to December 31, 1921.) Annotated 1921. Mount Hope, C.Z., Panama Canal Press, 1922. 332 p.
TC774.U6 1921

In the early period, especially during the first ten years, the Canal Zone was governed almost entirely by the president with only the most rudimentary legislative underpinning. Consequently, executive orders played an abnormally large part in the governance. This work is a uniquely valuable and now rare compilation of those orders arranged in chronological sequence. (1)

76

Panama Canal. *Laws, statutes, etc.* Laws of the Canal Zone, Isthmus of Panama, enacted by the Isthmian Canal Commission, August 16, 1904, to March 31, 1914. Annotated 1921. Mount Hope, C.Z., Panama Canal Press, 1922. 322 p.
LL

The Isthmian Canal Commission exercised legislative powers in the zone delegated by the president, which were conferred on the president by an act of Congress which expired on March 4, 1905. Prior to March 4, 1905, it enacted 24 acts, several being quasi-constitutional in nature, setting up a structure of civil government. Thereafter, without legal authority, it issued ordinances dealing generally with matters of lesser importance. Both acts and ordinances had in fact the force of law in the zone and are compiled in this volume in chronological order. (1)

B. Annual Reports of the Isthmian Canal Commission

Section 7 of the Spooner Act of June 28, 1902, created the Isthmian Canal Commission which, exercising almost unlimited powers delegated by the president, built the canal and governed the Canal Zone—as well as the two largest cities in the Republic of Panama for purposes of sanitation, water supply, and health—from 1904 to 1914. The same section required annual reports to the president on progress and activities. These annual reports, eleven in number, constitute the mother lode of basic data used by all researchers in the Canal Zone history of the period. Only a small proportion of each report touches directly or indirectly on relations with Panama growing out of the Hay-Bunau Varilla Treaty, but that proportion which does is likely to be found in several different places so it is not always feasible to cite specific pages. The table of contents provides a fairly reliable indicator of what the reader can skip over if he is only interested in some particular facet. All the annual reports are worth at least skimming in their entirety if for no other reason than to get a general picture of the events of the time. (The first entry in this subdivision, 77, is different in kind from, and is not one of, the annual reports, but is included because of its relevance to the continuity of the story.) The annual reports are presented in chronological order.

77

U.S. *Isthmian Canal Commission, 1899–1902.* Report of the Isthmian Canal Commission, 1899–1901. Rear Admiral John G. Walker, United States Navy, President. Washington, Govt. Print. Off., 1901–2. 2 v. (535 p.) maps, plates. (57th Congress, 1st session. Senate. Doc. 54)

TC773.U5 1901

This pre-Spooner-Act Isthmian Canal Commission, despite the confusing similarity of name, had nothing to do with building the canal. Its sole mission was to make a study of all suggested possible sites and recommend "the most practicable and feasible route" for an interoceanic canal. After an exceedingly thorough and amply documented investigation, it recommended (p. 257–63) the route through Nicaragua. The deciding factor was cost. The French-owned New Panama Canal Company, which would have had to be bought out if the canal were to be built through Panama, was demanding an exorbitant price of $109,141,500. The Isthmian Canal Commission later reversed its own decision and recommended the Panama Route after the New Panama Canal Company reduced its asking price to $40,000,000. (1)

78

U.S. *Isthmian Canal Commission, 1904–1905.* Letter from the Secretary of War, transmitting the first annual report of the Isthmian Canal Commission. December 1, 1904. Washington, Govt. Print. Off., 1905. 246 p. ([U.S.] 58th Congress, 3d session. House. Doc. 226)   TC774.U5 1905a

Includes also the first annual and supplemental reports of Major-General George W. Davis, Governor of the Canal Zone, and Laws of the Canal Zone, Isthmus of Panama, enacted by the Isthmian Canal Commission.

The Isthmian Canal Commission created by the Spooner Act, and fleshed out by the Act of April 28, 1904 (33 Stat. 429), actually began

functioning in May 1904; this report covers its activities to December 1, 1904. It is largely concerned with organizational matters and a compilation of pertinent groundwork documents which have been published elsewhere. In form it is a letter of transmittal dated January 12, 1905, from the secretary of war to the president, which provides an opportunity to point out that the Isthmian Canal Commission reported to the president through the secretary of war who was made directly responsible for its supervision. The president in turn transmitted the report, in a letter dated January 13, 1905, to the Congress. The president's letter reveals his dissatisfaction with the ground rules for the commission and presages the later reorganizations which eventually placed all the powers of the commission with one man, Col. George Washington Goethals. (1)

79

U.S. *Isthmian Canal Commission, 1905–1914.* Annual Report of the Isthmian Canal Commission for the year ending December 1, 1905. Washington, Govt. Print. Off., 1905. 340 p. plates.

TC774.U52 1905

The Isthmian Canal Commission was reorganized effective April 1, 1905. This report covers its activities from that date to December 1, 1905, plus all laws, orders, and resolutions promulgated by the preceding commission between December 1, 1904, and April 1, 1905. Relations with Panama are mentioned in several places, perhaps the most significant being at p. 47–53. (1)

80

—— Annual report of the Isthmian Canal Commission for the year ending December 1, 1906. Washington, Govt. Print. Off., 1907. 153 p. ([U.S.] 59th Congress, 2d session. House. Doc. 444)   TC774.U52 1906

Most of the material touching on relations with Panama is found in the first several pages and at p. 41–45. Attention should be called to p. 18: "Questions involving the power of sovereignty in the Canal Zone conferred upon the United States by Panama have from time to time come up for discussion, and this power has become more clearly defined." (1)

81

—— Annual report of the Isthmian Canal Commission for the fiscal year ended June 30, 1907. Washington, Govt. Print. Off., 1907. xiv, 239 p. fold. col. map, plates (part fold.)

TC774.U52 1907

Effective April 1, 1907, Pres. Theodore Roosevelt appointed the third and last commission with virtually all real power concentrated in the chairman, Colonel Goethals. (All three were essentially the same commission, distinguishable only by changes in personnel and operating directives.) The first three years had been a time of preparation; the next seven, under the third commission, would see the canal finished and the end of the temporary commission form of government. Material in this report specifically designated "Relations with Panama" is found at p. 146–52, but material of the same nature is also to be found scattered throughout. (1)

82

——Annual report of the Isthmian Canal Commission for the fiscal year ended June 30, 1908. Washington, Govt. Print. Off., 1908. xvi, 358 p. fold. col. maps, plans (part fold.), plates (part fold.) TC774.U52 1908

By 1908 organizational growing pains within the zone were over, and relations with Panama had settled into a quiet period. The latter subject is hardly mentioned in this report except in four paragraphs on p. 256 beginning with: "Almost all of the questions discussed with the officials of the Republic of Panama during the year either grew out of the provisions of the canal treaty and subsequent agreements between the United States and Panama, including the authority of the United States to do sanitary work in the cities of Panama and Colón, or arose from the proximity of the zone and Panama." One of the specific questions discussed was the transfer of old government records from the zone to Panama. (1)

83

——Annual report of the Isthmian Canal Commission for the fiscal year ended June 30, 1909. Washington, Govt. Print. Off., 1909. xvi, 357 p. fold. col. maps, plans (part fold.), plates (part fold.) TC774.U52 1909

Relations with Panama were said to continue to be satisfactory, p. 26 and p. 257–58. Specific mention is made, inter alia, of U.S. "observation" of the Panamanian presidential election in 1908, and some question arises concerning violation in the zone of the immigration laws of the republic. (1)

84

——Annual report of the Isthmian Canal Commission for the fiscal year ended June 30, 1910. Washington, Govt. Print. Off., 1910. xxii, 443 p. fold. col. maps, plates (part fold.) ([U.S.] 61st Congress, 3d session, House. Doc. 1030) TC774.U52 1910

Relations with Panama were said to continue to be satisfactory, p. 364–65. Specific mention is made, inter alia, of the stationing of zone police at Nombre de Dios in the republic, the construc-

tion of a railroad from Panama City to David in the republic (which was never done), and the enforcement of the executive decree of Panama prohibiting the recruitment of labor in the cities of Panama and Colón. (1)

85

——Annual report of the Isthmian Canal Commission for the fiscal year ended June 30, 1911. Washington, Govt. Print. Off., 1911. xxii, 581 p. fold. col. maps, plates. TC774.U52 1911

See p. 1–2, p. 48–56, and p. 414–15. Increasing concern is evidenced, as the canal nears completion, about private land title claims of Panamanian nationals. Need for revision of the criminal law and both criminal and civil procedural codes is mentioned (the substantive civil code of Panama continued to be applied in the zone until 1933) but no recommendations were to be made "until the policy of the United States with reference to the Canal Zone is determined."

Relations with Panama were said to continue to be satisfactory. Specific mention is made, inter alia, of the arrest of Americans by Panamanian police officers both in the zone and in the republic, extradition, the infringement in the Canal Zone of trade marks registered in Panama, the survey and demarcation of permanent boundaries of the Canal Zone, and the suppression of gambling and the white slave traffic in Panama City and Colón. (1)

86

——Annual report of the Isthmian Canal Commission for the fiscal year ended June 30, 1912. Washington, Govt. Print. Off., 1912. xxii, 619 p. fold. col. maps, plates. TC774.U52 1912

See p. 58–64 and p. 455–528. A decision having been made to depopulate the zone except for employees (including military) and contractors of the U.S. government, a census was taken as of February 1, 1912, to determine how many persons would be affected (see entry 29). The total population was found to be 62,810, of whom 42,174 were eligible for continued residence. (Almost no natives of the isthmus were employed in building the canal.)

Attention was again called to the necessity of revision of Canal Zone laws: "The zone is now governed by laws of Colombia, of Panama, by executive orders of the president, and ordinances of the commission."

Relations with Panama were said to continue to be satisfactory. Specific mention is made of several relatively minor matters requiring negotiations similar to those noted in previous years. The report of the department of law (p. 515–528) probes deeper than in any previous annual report into the conflict between the American (common law) and the Panamanian (civil law) legal systems. (The eventual virtually complete displacement of the civil law in the zone is one of the seeds of the present controversy between the two countries. For further examination of this subject, see entry 12a.) (1)

87
——Annual report of the Isthmian Canal Commission for the fiscal year ended June 30, 1913. Washington, Govt. Print. Off., 1913. xxi, 633 p. fold. col. maps, plates.   TC774.U52 1913

See p. 61–67 and p. 459–525. The most important event during this fiscal year was the passage of the Panama Canal Act of August 24, 1912 (37 Stat. 560), which replaced the Spooner Act as the organic law of the Canal Zone and provided for the establishment of a "permanent" government whenever, in the president's judgment, the canal should be sufficiently near completion.

The next most important was the Executive Order of December 5, 1912, which, pursuant to section 3 of the Panama Canal Act, eliminated all private land titles in the zone by declaring all land, and land under water, in the entire zone necessary for the "construction, maintenance, operation, sanitation, or protection of the Panama Canal." The language in quotation marks is taken directly from article II of the Hay-Bunau Varilla Treaty. (Panamanians have never admitted that such action was really necessary for the purposes enumerated, and that is another of the seeds of the present controversy.) As "depopulation" was the principal legal activity during the year, "the prosecuting attorney devoted his time almost exclusively to the adjustment of land claims. . . ."

Relations with Panama were said to continue to be satisfactory. Specific mention is made, inter alia, of the superior rights of the United States under the treaty to use the rivers and streams of the republic, the deportation to the republic of ex-convicts, and certain reciprocal adjustments of customs and tax matters. (1)

88
——Annual report of the Isthmian Canal Commission for the fiscal year ended June 30, 1914. Washington, Govt. Print. Off., 1914. xxii, 603 p. plates.   TC774.U52 1914

See p. 54–62, p. 511–23, and p. 553–601. Under the Executive Order of January 27, 1914, in conformity with section 4 of the Panama Canal Act, the Isthmian Canal Commission was abolished, and the new form of government prescribed for the zone in the Panama Canal Act was instituted as of April 1, 1914.

Relations with Panama were said to continue to be satisfactory. Specific mention is made, inter alia, of jurisdiction of the United States over

islands and peninsulas in the republic formed by the waters of Gatun Lake, enforcement of the Panamanian exclusion laws in the Canal Zone, the deportation of an American in the city of Panama charged with fraudulently representing himself as an attorney licensed to practice in the Canal Zone courts, and several of the same minor irritants and adminstrative adjustments mentioned in previous reports. (1)

C. Congressional Documents, Reports, and Hearings

Prefacing this subdivision, three points need to be noted briefly.

First, the word *selective* in the title of the bibliography applies to this subdivision perhaps even more than to others. If every issuance that could be included under this heading were actually listed, the sheer mass of material would be suffocating and far in excess of any perceived need.

Second, in a chronological compilation of congressional issuances on Panama Canal treaty matters there is a natural divide which is marked by President Johnson's commitment in 1964 to negotiate a new treaty in which the basic concepts of the 1903 treaty would be abrogated. All congressional issuances since 1964 have taken cognizance, explicitly or implicitly, of the fact that treaty relations with Panama have entered a new and volatile phase, the outcome of which cannot be foreseen but which is certain to have far-reaching consequences.

Third, several of the entries in other subdivisions of genus II have been published in the form of congressional issuances, citation to which is made as part of the entry. They are not repeated in this subdivision, which is chronologically arranged by the development of the events, not by imprint dates.

89
U.S. *Congress. House. Select Committee on a Canal or Railroad Between the Atlantic and Pacific Oceans.* Canal or railroad between the Atlantic and Pacific Oceans. [Report] February 20, 1849. [Washington, 1849] 678 p. fold. maps, fold. plates. ([U.S.] 30th Congress, 2d session. House. Report 145)   TC773.U3 1849
                                                  Serial no. 546
Presented by John A. Rockwell to accompany Jt. Res. no. 42.

This is not the earliest fruit of congressional interest in interoceanic communication (as noted on p. 3), but it is, for all practical purposes, a good place to start, being an interesting, cumulative, and comprehensive miscellany of ideas and projects to date taken from many disparate sources, and having its immediate impetus in the geopolitical imperative of "the recent acquisition of California, and the recognition and establishment of the right of the United States to the Oregon territory. . . ." The best part of the report (p. 506–90) is the article by a French engineer, Napoleon Garella, who argued that the French government should promptly take the lead in building a canal. He was severely critical of the idea of building a railroad (construction of which was begun in May 1850 by an American company) on the grounds that a railroad in being would forever obstruct the building of a canal. History has invalidated his prophecy. (2)

90

U.S. *Dept. of State.* Report of the Secretary of State with accompanying correspondence in relation to the proposed interoceanic canal between the Atlantic and Pacific oceans. Transmitted to the Senate in obediance to a resolution. Washington, Govt. Print. Off., 1880. 152 p. (U.S. 46th Congress, 2d session. Senate. Ex. doc. 112)

TC773.U47 1880
Serial no. 1885

March 9, 1880.—Referred to the Committee on Foreign Relations and ordered to be printed.

A comprehensive report, against the background of the Clayton-Bulwer Treaty, of U.S. negotiations on the subject with various Latin American countries and with Great Britain. In the light of hindsight, probably the most significant thing about this document was the following short sentence in President Hayes's introductory letter to the Senate: "The policy of this country is a canal under American control." This document should be read in connection with entries 42 and 95. (1)

91

U.S. *Congress. House. Select Committee on Interoceanic Ship Canal.* Interoceanic ship canal. Testimony taken before the Select Committee on Interoceanic Ship Canal in regard to the selection of a suitable route for the construction of an interoceanic ship canal across the American isthmus. Washington, Govt. Print. Off., 1881. 129 p. ([U.S.] 46th Congress, 3d session. House. Misc. doc. 16)

TC773.U3 1881
Serial no. 1981

The testimony of Ferdinand de Lesseps, who was on the verge of organizing the first French

canal company with the objective of building a sea-level canal across the Isthmus of Panama, commences on p. 50. While the hearings were concerned mostly with engineering and commercial questions, and the relative advantages of the Nicaraguan and Panamanian routes, some notice was taken (p. 111–17) of the rights and responsibilities of the United States under international law arising from the Treaty of 1846 with New Granada and the Monroe Doctrine. (2)

92

———The Monroe Doctrine. Report (to accompany H. Res. 236). [Washington, Govt. Print. Off., 1885] 9 p. ([U.S.] 46th Congress, 3d session. House. Report no. 390)

TC773.U3 1885
Serial no. 1983

Submitted by Mr. King.
Ordered to be printed, March 3, 1881. Ordered to be reprinted January 5, 1885.

An unequivocal statement by the Select Committee on Interoceanic Ship Canal that any canal connecting the Caribbean Sea to the Pacific Ocean, by whomever built and under whatever ostensible management, must be under the ultimate control of the United States. (1)

93

U.S. *Dept. of State.* The Clayton-Bulwer Treaty and the Monroe Doctrine. A letter from the Secretary of State to the Minister of the United States at London, dated May 8, 1882, with sundry papers and documents explanatory of the same, selected from the archives of the Department of State. Washington, Govt. Print. Off., 1882. 203 p. (1) [U.S.] 47th Congress, 1st session. Senate. Ex. doc. no. 194)

JX1425.A3 1882
Serial no. 1991

An exhaustive review of the circumstances surrounding the Clayton-Bulwer Treaty with argumentation intended to persuade the government of Great Britain that its premises are inapplicable to the changed conditions and that it would be in the best interests of both countries for any canal which might be built in the future to be under the unrestricted control of the United States. This document should be read in connection with entries 90 and 95. (1)

94

U.S. *Bureau of Naval Personnel.* Report of historical and technical information relating to the problem of interoceanic communication by way of the American isthmus, by John T. Sullivan, lieutenant, U.S. Navy. By order of the Bureau of Navigation, Navy Department. Washington, Govt. Print. Off., 1883. 219 p. maps (part fold.), plates.

TC773.U24 1883
Serial no. 2112

Bibliography: p. 214–219.

Issued also as House Ex. doc. 107, [U.S.] 47th Congress, 2d session.

One more account for the record of the transisthmian canal saga to date, replete with maps, charts, and engineering data, competently done and well researched, but largely redundant. In hindsight, and in the context of this bibliography, the most contributive part of the report consists of the keen observations of the author concerning the Wyse surveys (p. 94 et seq.) and the unsuccessful efforts of the French canal promoters to avoid having to buy out the previously acquired rights of the Panama Railroad Company. (3)

95

U.S. *Dept. of State*. Message from the President of the United States, transmitting, in response to the Senate resolution of the 18th instant, a report of the Secretary of State and accompanying papers relating to the treaty between the United States and Great Britain, signed April 19, 1850. [Washington, Govt. Print. Off., 1884] 15 p. ([U.S.] 48th Congress, 1st session. Senate. Ex. doc. no. 26)

J66
Serial no. 2162

December 19, 1883.—Read and ordered to lie on the table and be printed.

More on the Clayton-Bulwer Treaty. This document should be read in connection with entries 90 and 93. (1)

96

McCreary, James B. The construction or control of interoceanic canals at the Isthmus of Darien and in Central America by European governments. Mr. McCreary, from the Committee on Foreign Affairs, made the following report (to accompany Senate Res. 122). [Washington, Govt. Print. Off., 1889] 28 p. ([U.S.] 50th Congress, 2d session. House. Report no. 4167)

J66
Serial no. 2675

March 2, 1889.—Referred to the House Calendar and ordered to be printed.

This report came at a time when the privately financed (French) Old Panama Canal Company had obviously failed, and its purpose was to support a joint resolution warning the government of France that any move to take over the project would be considered a violation of the Monroe Doctrine. It includes a minority opinion expressing a contrary view. Contains interesting

commentaries on the Treaty of 1846, the Clayton-Bulwer Treaty, and the proper role of Congress in foreign affairs. (1)

97

U.S. *Congress. House. Committee on Interstate and Foreign Commerce*. Hearings before the Committee on Interstate and Foreign Commerce of the House of Representatives on New Panama Canal Company, the Maritime Company, and the Nicaragua Canal Company (Grace-Eyre-Craigan Syndicate). Held January 17, 18, 19, 20, and 25, 1899. Washington, Govt. Print. Off., 1899. 191 p. ([U.S.] 56th Congress, 1st session. Senate. Doc. no. 50)

TC773.U3 1899
Serial no. 3848

December 20, 1899.—Presented by Mr. Morgan and ordered to be printed.

These hearings were apparently called on the initiative of William Nelson Cromwell, general counsel for the privately refinanced (French) New Panama Canal Company, before a mostly hostile committee for the purpose of taking testimony on the rival Panamanian and Nicaraguan canal routes. The New Panama Canal Company had about come to the end of its rope at this time and was desperately trying to preserve its credibility in the face of increasing signs that the U.S. government might throw its weight behind the Nicaraguan route. Though the New Panama Canal Company had completed, by its own estimate, about two-fifths of the projected canal, it had run out of money, and prospects for raising the enormous additional funds that would be needed were bleak.

This document is only a record of testimony and does not express any conclusion. While the weight of the testimony seems to favor the Nicaraguan route, Cromwell probably accomplished his purpose of raising enough doubt (or hope) to keep the Panamanian route alive while he maneuvered in other ways to rally support for it. If the hearings made anything clear, it was that neither route would ever be completed with anything less than the complete commitment of the U.S. government. (2)

98

U.S. Congress. Senate. Committee on Interoceanic Canals. Interoceanic canal. [Report to accompany the bill (H.R. 2538) to provide for the construction of a canal connecting the waters of the Atlantic and Pacific oceans. Washington, Govt. Print. Off., 1900] 144 p. ([U.S.] 56th Congress, 1st session. Senate. Report no. 1337)

TC773.U35 1900

Calendar no. 1289.

Submitted by Mr. John T. Morgan. Ordered printed, May 16, 1900. ——Interoceanic Canal.

Supplemental report. [Washington, Govt. Print. Off., 1900?] ([U.S.] 56th Congress, 2d session. Senate. Report no. 1337, pt. 3) J66

Serial no. 4063

Submitted by Mr. Morgan. Ordered to be printed Dec. 18, 1900. ——Interoceanic Canal. Additional report. [Washington, Govt. Print. Off., 1901] xcvi, 384 p. diagr. ([U.S.] 56th Congress, 2d session. Senate. Report no. 1337, pt. 4) TC773.U35

Submitted by Mr. Morgan. Ordered printed Jan. 7, 1901.

The bill which this multi-part and wide-ranging report was intended to accompany was sponsored in the House by U.S. Congressman Hepburn and in the Senate by Senator Morgan, both zealous advocates of the Nicaraguan route, and authorizes the president to construct a canal through the territory of Nicaragua and Costa Rica, without mentioning Panama. Nevertheless, Panama is injected into the report forcefully and at length, primarily, it would seem, at the insistence of Senator Hanna. Senator Morgan tried to dismiss the Panamanian route and the propositions of the (French) New Panama Canal Company with ridicule and contempt (see reference, for example, in part 4 at p. ix, to the shaky financial condition of the New Panama Canal Company as previously exposed in Senate document 50, entry 97) but Senator Hanna would not permit him to do so. That is the essence of the internal drama of this report.

In international law, its significance lies in the bold statement, on the very first page, that the control of any canal connecting the Atlantic and Pacific oceans, wherever or by whomever it may be built, must rest with the United States. That position is announced even more emphatically in part 3 of the report, p. 1, which cites the appropriation act of March 3, 1899 (30 Stat. 1150) authorizing the president to determine the most practicable route for a canal and place it under the control of the United States. The Act of March 3, 1899, on the last day of the session, was crucial not only in international law but also in that it revived consideration of the Panamanian route at the last possible minute. The investigative commission that was created pursuant thereto, in the Act of June 10, 1899, by President McKinley, is the same that later became known as the second Walker Commission (entry 77) and which recommended, in a final report of January 18, 1902, the construction of a canal at Panama. (1)

99

——Report of the Senate Committee on Interoceanic Canals on the proposed ship canals through the American isthmus connecting the continents of North and South America. Wash-ington, Govt. Print. Off., 1901. 551 p. diagr. ([U.S.] 57th Congress, 1st session. Senate. Rep. no. 1) TC773.U35 1901

Serial no. 4256

Calendar no. 3.
Ordered printed, December 12, 1901.

This report was intended to accompany S. 451 (57th Congress, 1st session), which, like H.R. 2538 (entry 98), had for its purpose the construction of a canal through Lake Nicaragua and made no mention of Panama. The report, however, delves deeply once again into the whole history of interoceanic projects, including necessarily those involving Panama. Though the pro-Nicaragua bias of Senator Morgan is evidenced on almost every page and there is much repetition, the report is still a useful compendium of documents and testimony and is expository of the increasingly proprietary attitude of the United States toward any canal. It has one curiously anachronistic feature in that much of its energy is directed at the iniquities of the Clayton-Bulwer Treaty which was at that moment just on the verge of supersession by the Hay-Pauncefote Treaty. (2)

100

U.S. *Isthmian Canal Commisssion, 1899–1902.* Report of the Isthmian Canal Commission. Message from the President of the United States, transmitting the report . . . upon the proposition of the New Panama Canal Company to sell and dispose of all its rights, property, and unfinished work to the United States. January 20, 1902.—Read; referred to the Committee on Interoceanic Canals and ordered to be printed. [Washington, Govt. Print. Off., 1902] 10 p. ([U.S.] 57th Congress, 1st session. Senate. Doc. 123) TC773.U5 1902

Serial no. 4230

Supplementary to the *Report* of the Isthmian Canal Commission, 1899–1901, issued as Senate doc. 54, [U.S.] 57th Congress, first session (entry 77), in which the index to the present work was printed (p. 535).

This supplementary report, with index, is found also in the *Report* of the Commission, 1899–1901, published with additional material in 1904 and issued as Senate doc. 222, [U.S.] 58th Congress, 2d session (p. 673–681).

It would be impossible to exaggerate the importance of this ten-page document. It was the turning point in the long fight between advocates of the Nicaraguan route and of the Panamanian route. For the first time an official investigatory commission unequivocally recommended the Panamanian route. Though Senator Morgan and his followers supporting the Nicaraguan route still commanded a majority in the Committee on Interoceanic Canals, their position had been fatally undermined, as shown in entry 101.

This report contains the following passage (p. 9) which is often cited by those who resist any weakening of rights granted to the United States in the Hay-Bunau Varilla Treaty:

The grant must not be for a term of years, but in perpetuity, and a strip of territory from ocean to ocean of sufficient width must be placed under the control of the United States. In this strip the United States must have the right to enforce police regulations, preserve order, protect property rights, and exercise such other powers as are appropriate and necessary. (1)

101
U.S. *Congress. Senate. Committee on Interoceanic Canals.* Report, with the views of the minority [favoring the Panama route] (To accompany H.R. 3110.) [Washington, U.S. Govt. Print. Off., 1902] 2 pts. in 1 v. ([U.S.] 57th Congress, 1st session. Senate. Report no. 783)

TC774.U35 1902
Serial no. 4260

Contents: pt. 1. Isthmian canal. March 19, 1902 ... Mr. Morgan ... submitted the following report, with the views of the minority—pt. 2. Interoceanic canals. May 31, 1902 ... Mr. Kittredge ... submitted the following additional views of the minority.

Under the heading "Additional Views of the Minority," the following paragraph synthesizes the spirit of this report and shows which way the wind was beginning to blow:

The majority of the committee reportedly favored the bill for the construction of the canal by the Nicaragua route, together with the voluminous evidence of the members of the Commission and of other witnesses who have appeared before the committee; but the action of the majority in favor of the Nicaragua route is wholly contrary to the report of the Isthmian Canal Commission and to the testimony of its members before this committee.

A little further on another paragraph is worth quoting in part because of its unintentionally revealing commentary on the herculean magnitude of the task attempted in this bibliography, even if only the challenge of selectivity be considered: "Upon no subject which has ever been before Congress has so much been written and spoken as upon the isthmian canal. The mass of printed material alone is so huge that it would be impossible for Senators even to examine it...."

Written in 1902, this statement takes no account of the additional printed matter which was poured out in the subsequent seventy-four years. (1)

102
U.S. *Dept. of State.* Letters from the Colombian Minister [with proposed convention for the construction of interoceanic canal by Panama route, letter from the Nicaraguan Minister with draft of treaty touching interoceanic canal through Nicaragua] etc. May 16, 1902.—Ordered to be printed. [Washington, Govt. Print. Off., 1902] 25 p. ([U.S.] 57th Congress, 1st session. House. Doc. no. 611) TC773.U47 1902

Serial no. 4377

In this collection of correspondence and other documents, Secretary of State John Hay undertakes to inform Congressman Hepburn, chairman of the House Committee on Interstate and Foreign Commerce, of the state of negotiations with Colombia and Nicaragua, respectively, concerning the decision of the United States to build an interoceanic canal. Drafts of conventions with both countries are included. As of mid-1902 it was clear that the construction of such a canal was no longer a question of if but simply a question of where and under what conditions. Colombia seemed ready to waive the restrictions in the Wyse Concession against alienation of the concessionary rights to a foreign government, but continued to insist on an explicit declaration of Colombian sovereignty over the territory concerned. Likewise, the draft convention with Nicaragua provided that: "The sovereignty of Nicaragua and the laws of the Republic not inconsistent with this convention shall be in full force in the Nicaraguan territory comprised in the canal district." (1)

103
——Use by the United States of a military force in the internal affairs of Colombia, etc. [under the treaty of 1846] Message from the President of the United States, transmitting, in response to Senate resolution no. 73 of January 22, 1904, reports from the acting Secretary of State and the Secretary of the Navy, with accompanying papers. [Washington, Govt. Print. Off., 1904] 240 p. ([U.S.] 58th Congress, 2d session. Senate. Doc. 143) F1566.U579

Serial no. 4589

The edition cited consists of 337 pages and includes as an appendix a reprint of *Correspondence Relating to the Military Occupation of Bays of Panama and Colon, etc.,* issued as Senate doc. 10 of the [U.S.] 58th Congress, special session.

There is a kind of watershed between this and the preceding entry because in the meantime the basic factual situation had been dramatically altered by the Panamanian Revolution of November 1903, followed almost immediately by U.S. recognition and the Hay-Bunau Varilla Treaty. The Senate resolution to which this message from the president is responsive was obviously drawn up by senators who felt that President Roosevelt acted wrongly in the crisis and in violation of international law. By answering the questions as posed, the president was virtually forced to concede that all previous military interventions had been in support of the central government, pursuant to the Treaty of 1846, whereas the last had had a totally opposite effect.

For further enlightenment as to the sense of the Senate with respect to the resolution and a vigorous defense of the presidential actions, see *Congressional Record,* 58th Congress, 2d session, v. 38, January 22, 1904, p. 1023–36. (1)

104
———Constitution of the Republic of Panama. Message from the President of the United States, transmitting, in response to the second request of the Senate Resolution of February 18, 1904, a report from the Secretary of State submitting a translation of the Constitution of the Republic of Panama as promulgated on the afternoon of February 16, 1904; and also a copy of a dispatch from the Legation of the United States at Panama dated February 22, 1904 reporting the inauguration of the President of Panama and the personnel of his cabinet. Washington, Govt. Print. Off., 1904. 26 p. ([U.S.] 58th Congress, 2d session. Senate. Doc. no. 208)   JL1643.1904a.A5
                                           Serial no. 4591
March 16, 1904—Read; referred to the Committee on Foreign Relations and ordered to be printed.

This is a verbatim translation of the first constitution of the new Republic of Panama. Its chief significance, for purposes of this bibliography, lies in article 136:

The Government of the United States of America may intervene in any part of the Republic of Panama to reestablish public peace and constitutional order in the event of their being disturbed, provided that that nation shall, by public treaty, assume or have assumed the obligation of guaranteeing the independence and sovereignty of this Republic.

Ten days later the Hay-Bunau Varilla Treaty provided in article I that, "The United States guarantees and will maintain the independence of the Republic of Panama." Thus, in effect, the United States accepted the voluntary offer of the Republic of Panama to make itself a dependency of the United States. Times have changed and both articles have since been repealed, but that is the way it was in the beginning and for a good many years thereafter (until 1936). (1)

105
Bristow, Joseph L. Report of Joseph L. Bristow, Special Panama Railroad Commissioner, to the Secretary of War, June 24, 1905. Published by Office of Administration, Isthmian Canal Affairs. Washington, Govt. Print. Off., 1906. 421 p.

fold. illus. ([U.S.] 59th Congress, 1st session. Senate. Doc. no. 429)   HE2830.P2A4 1906
                                           Serial no. 4919
On January 13, 1905, Mr. Bristow was appointed by the president to make a thorough investigation of "present trade conditions and freight rates," and other matters, "for the purpose of determining the best policy to be pursued in the management of the Panama Railroad Company." The underlying reason for such an investigation lay in the obvious fact that the railroad, which had been the principal means of interoceanic communication since 1855, would soon be supplanted in its principal function by the canal. Remembering that the railroad also owned and operated a fleet of ships, what should be its priorities and its relationship to the canal? Besides offering a practicable set of recommendations, this report contains a useful recapitulation of the various contracts and modifications thereof between the railroad company and Colombia, all of which were subsequently subsumed in the Hay-Bunau Varilla Panama Canal Treaty. (2)

106
U.S. *War Dept.* Isthmian Canal. Message from the President of the United States, transmitting certain papers to accompany his message of January 8, 1906. January 11, 1906.—Read; referred to the Committee on Interoceanic Canals, and ordered to be printed. Washington, Govt. Print. Off., 1906. 91 p. ([U.S.] 59th Congress, 1st session. Senate. Doc. 127, pt. 2)
                                           TC774.U52
                                           Serial no. 4919
Contents: Letter from the Secretary of War to the President concerning the charges against the Isthmian Canal Commission contained in an article [by Poultney Bigelow] in the "Independent," a weekly publication [with Exhibits A–G]— Our Mismanagement at Panama, by Poultney Bigelow.

This document is of interest chiefly as an example of the lengths to which the president and secretary of war felt it was necessary to go to refute the scurrilous charges of irresponsible journalists, so as to avoid undermining public confidence in the canal-building project. The document is also of some value for conveying an authentic feel of the time and place (1906 in Colón). Insofar as it touches on the early legal history of the Canal Zone, it accurately reflects the mixture of languages and legal systems. Two of the three justices of the Canal Zone Supreme Court were bilingual in English and Spanish; in interpersonal civil relations the Spanish civil law was applied; in procedural and criminal matters the American common law was applied; most of the defendants and litigants were in fact, contrary to the impression left by Mr. Bigelow, English-speaking persons from the British West Indies. (3)

107

U.S. *Congress. Senate. Committee on Interoceanic Canals.* Investigation of Panama Canal matters. Hearings before the Committee on Interoceanic Canals of the United States Senate in the matter of the Senate Resolution adopted January 9, 1906, providing for an investigation of matters relating to the Panama Canal, etc. Washington, Govt. Print. Off., 1907, 4 v. fold. illus. ([U.S.] 59th Congress, 2d session. Senate. Doc. no. 401)   TC774.U6 1906ib
Serial no. 5097–5100

These hearings constitute the most exhaustive review to date (1906) of "all matters relating to the Panama Canal and the government of the Canal Zone and the management of the Panama Railroad Company" and were conducted pursuant to a Senate resolution of January 9, 1906. For anyone who has the time and sufficient interest, a full reading would be most edifying and rewarding. It would be impracticable to attempt to cite the most significant passages as that would involve too many subtle value judgments. Two points of interest will be mentioned, however. First, some basic questions of international law, sovereignty, relations with Panama, and the validity of the government in the Canal Zone are touched on, passim, in the testimony of General Davis, first governor of the zone, p. 2161–2410. Second, the testimony of William Nelson Cromwell, p. 1041–1249 and p. 3059–3207, is noteworthy. As unadorned, and often understated, fact, it describes how this one remarkable lawyer (though assisted independently, in his own way, by the French engineer Bunau-Varilla) brought the Panama Canal into existence against impossible odds while simultaneously playing many parts (representing, for example, the Panama Railroad Company, the [French] New Panama Canal Company, various banks, at times the governments of Colombia, Panama, and the United States, and himself, as stockholder and claimant of enormous legal fees). (1)

108

——Refusal of William Nelson Cromwell to answer certain questions, etc. . . . Extracts from the hearings on Interoceanic Canals [February 26–May 11, 1906. Washington, Govt. Print. Off., 1906] 58 p. ([U.S.] 59th Congress, 1st session. Senate. Doc. 457)   TC774.U6 1906j
Serial no. 4915
Presented by Mr. Millard.
Ordered printed May 25, 1906.
Includes "Memorandum as to privilege of counsel to testify when called as a witness," submitted by J. T. Morgan.

This document, which consists in large part of excerpts from Senate document 401 (entry 107), was printed at the insistence of Sen. J. T. Morgan, an advocate of the Nicaraguan canal route, to enter on the record—and vent his indignation at—what he held to be the illegal refusal of William Nelson Cromwell, who supported the Panamanian route, to answer a great many of the questions propounded to him during the hearings. It is a memorable fencing match in which the resourceful senator from Alabama was unable to break through the defense of the international lawyer. (3)

109

Government of Canal Zone. Congressional Record, [U.S.] 60th Congress, 1st session, v. 42, pt. 4, March 19, 1908: 3582–3592.
J11.R5, v. 42, pt. 4

The Act of April 28, 1904 (33 Stat. 429) provided for "the temporary government of the Canal Zone at Panama" but the powers of government granted to the president thereunder expired on March 4, 1905, and were never renewed (until, retroactively, the Panama Canal Act of 1912). After March 4, 1905, the president continued to govern and "legislate" for the Canal Zone, mostly through the agency of the Isthmian Canal Commission, without, his critics alleged, any legal authority.

This passage from the *Congressional Record* concerns the following resolution introduced by Mr. Ryan of New York:

Resolved, That the President of the United States be, and he is hereby, requested to inform this House, if not incompatible with the public interests, by what authority of law he has exercised the functions of government in the Panama Canal Zone since the date of the expiration of the Fifty-eighth Congress, or by what right or authority the executive, legislative, and judicial functions in the Zone have been performed since that date.

The resolution was duly passed on March 19, 1908. (2)

110

Civil government in Canal Zone. Congressional Record, [U.S.] 60th Congress, 1st session, v. 42, pt. 5, April 4, 1908: 4387–4388.
J11.R5, v. 42, pt. 5

This passage from the *Congressional Record* is the reply of Pres. Theodore Roosevelt to the resolution quoted in the immediately preceding entry. (2)

111

U.S. *Congress. House. Committee on Foreign Affairs.* The story of Panama. Hearings on the Rainey resolution before the Committee on Foreign

Affairs of the House of Representatives. Washington, Govt. Print. Off., 1913. 736 p.

F1566.5.U3

Henry D. Flood, chairman.

Hearings 1–4: Jan. 26 and Feb. 9, Feb. 9 and 12, Feb. 13 and 14, Feb. 15, 16, and 20, 1912, preceded by "Statement of Frank D. Pavey," Feb. 19, 1913, including "Statement on Behalf of Historical Truth," by P. Bunau-Varilla, etc., etc. (p. 3–44).

"Arbitration between Messrs. Sullivan and Cromwell and La Compagnie Nouvelle du Canal de Panama, tr. by Henry N. Hall. March 1911" (Mr. Cromwell's brief) p. 193–298.

"The Panama Libel Suit": p. 299–311.

This is surely the most fascinating, and quite possibly the most illuminating, of all the documents churned out over the years by the Congress on the subject of the Panama Canal. In form this document is a series of hearings pursuant to the following politically partisan resolution introduced in the House by Congressman Henry T. Rainey, Democrat, of Illinois (later Speaker of the House):

Whereas a former President of the United States [Theodore Roosevelt] has declared that he "took" Panama from the Republic of Colombia without consulting Congress; and

Whereas the Republic of Colombia has ever since petitioned this country to submit to The Hague tribunal the legal and equitable question whether such taking was in accordance with or in violation of the treaty then existing between the two countries, and also whether such taking was in accordance with or in violation of the well-established principles of the law of nations; and

Whereas the Government of the United States professes its desire to submit all international controversies to arbitration and has conducted treaties with many other nations agreeing to submit all legal questions to arbitration, but has steadfastly refused arbitration to the Republic of Colombia; Therefore be it

Resolved, That the Committee on Foreign Affairs of the House of Representatives be, and the same hereby is, directed to inquire into the same; send for books, papers, and documents; summon witnesses; take testimony; and report the same, with its opinions and conclusions thereon, to this House with all convenient speed.

In the course of inquiring, the committee turned up such a wealth of sensitive and revealing inside material on hitherto hidden manipulations in the "story of Panama" that they cannot even be summarized in an annotation. The most that can be done is to mention two main subjects—the arbitration between the law firm of Sullivan & Cromwell and their client, the (French) New Panama Canal Company over how much their services were worth, and the so-called Panama Libel Suit involving charges that relatives of Taft, Roosevelt, and other highly placed Republicans had profited improperly by the $40-million payment to the New Panama Canal Company—and the ancillary hornets' nest

stirred up between Cromwell and Bunau-Varilla over who was most responsible for the successful outcome of the fight for the Panamanian route.

For purposes of this bibliography, the significance of these matters is not the issues themselves but the information revealed in the heat of the arguments.

In a typewritten insert in this document (between p. 10 and 11) reference is made to a typed supplementary statement written by Bunau-Varilla in 1938 "to be found in the Division of Manuscripts of the Library of Congress." See entry 222a.

To round out and balance the picture, reference should also be made to the judgment of one of Roosevelt's biographers—*Theodore Roosevelt* by Lord Charnwood, published by Atlantic Monthly Press, Boston, 1923—at p. 143–44:

Meanwhile one newspaper interested in the matter, quietly dropping the original charges, employed an enterprising member of its staff to inquire into the intrigues carried on in America by an agent of the French Company, the supposed connection of Roosevelt with those intrigues leading to the further suggestion that the whole story throughout was a wicked conspiracy of his against Colombia. The evidence which this good gentleman got together is to be found printed in imposing bulk in the report of a Congressional Committee [entry 111, *The Story of Panama*]. The whole mass of it is totally worthless, depending as it does upon the evidence which the said agent of the French Company unsuccessfully put forward in an arbitration in Paris for the purpose of magnifying the services which he had rendered to that Company. It should never again be referred to as an authority for anything. (1)

112

U.S. *Treaties, etc.* Canal treaties. Executive documents presented to the United States Senate, together with proceedings by the Senate thereon relative to the Panama Canal. Washington, Govt. Print. Off., 1914. 84 p. ([U.S.] 63rd Congress, 2d session. Senate. Doc. no. 456)

JX1398.5.A5 1914c
TC774.U6 1914
Serial no. 6594

Submitted by Mr. Williams.

Contents: Clayton-Bulwer Treaty.—Hay-Pauncefote Treaty.—Senate Proceedings on the Treaty of 1900.—Treaty of 1901.—Ratification of Treaty of 1901.—Statement by Secretary Hay.—Hay-Herrán Treaty (with Colombia).—Hay-Bunau-Varilla Treaty (with Panama).

All the individual items in this collection had already, of course, been printed elsewhere, but it was the sense of the Senate, on March 23, 1914, that it would be convenient to have them published as one document in chronological order. Thus, in this document one may follow canal treaty developments from the Clayton-Bulwer Treaty with Great Britain to the Hay-

Bunau Varilla Treaty with Panama consecutively with no intervening and distracting extraneous material. (2)

113

U.S. *Dept. of State*. Diplomatic history of the Panama Canal. Correspondence relating to the negotiation and application of certain treaties on the subject of the construction of an interoceanic canal, and accompanying papers. Washington, Govt. Print. Off., 1914. 602 p. ([U.S.] 63rd Congress, 2d session. Senate. Doc. no. 474)

JXI398.6.A5 1914
Serial no. 6582

Includes a report of the Secretary of State, with papers relative to the construction of the Panama Canal.

A resolution of the Senate of April 14, 1914 requested the President, if not incompatible with the public interest, to cause to be transmitted to the Senate all information, papers, correspondence, messages, dispatches, and records in the Department of State relative to the superseding of the Clayton-Bulwer treaty by the so-called Hay-Pauncefote treaty (signed November eighteenth, nineteen hundred and one), from the beginning of negotiations to this date, and also relative to said Hay-Pauncefote treaty; and also similar information, papers, correspondence, messages, etc. relative to the Hay-Bunau Varilla treaty between the United States and Colombia [sic].

The above resolution offers an accurate enough description of the contents of this document. It is the first comprehensive coverage of the subject in a congressional issuance since Senate document 401 (entry 107) as well as the first to embrace the Hay-Bunau Varilla Treaty and the Panama Canal Act of 1912. Though a document of the utmost importance, it is somewhat marred by unaccountably erratic editing. Besides the bizarre identification of the Hay-Bunau Varilla Treaty as between the United States and Colombia, there is a typographical error on p. 543 which could be very confusing as it makes a letter from Bunau-Varilla to Secretary Hay which was written in 1904 appear to have been written in 1914. Much of the correspondence herein also appears in *Foreign Relations of the United States* (JX233.A3) for the appropriate year. (1)

114

U.S. *President, 1913–1921 (Wilson)*. Panama Canal tolls. Address of the President of the United States delivered at a joint session of the two houses of Congress, March 5, 1914. Washington, 1914. [2] p. ([U.S.] 63rd Congress, 2d session. House. Doc. no. 813)

HE537.9.17A4 1914b
Serial no. 6755

March 5, 1914.—Referred to the Committee on Interstate and Foreign Commerce and ordered to be printed.

Section 5 of the Panama Canal Act of 1912 contained a provision exempting from tolls "vessels engaged in the coastwide trade of the United States." As only U.S. flag ships could engage in such trade, this was clearly discriminatory and so, the British government contended, in violation of article III of the Hay-Pauncefote Treaty of 1901 which provided that the canal should be open to the vessels of all nations on terms of complete equality. President Wilson, in this address, requested the Congress to repeal that provision of the Panama Canal Act, and the Congress did so, though not without considerable opposition. In the view of many jurists, the government of Colombia made an equally good case that the Hay-Bunau Varilla Treaty was in violation of the Treaty of 1846. The contrasting responses to the British and Colombian protests make an interesting historical study (see entry 12a, p. 48). Colombia was eventually "compensated" in the Thomson-Urrutia Treaty (see entry 154).

For a full discussion of the international law issues raised by the conflict between the Panama Canal Act and the Hay-Pauncefote Treaty, see entry 3. (2)

115

U.S. *Congress. Senate. Committee on Interoceanic Canals*. Revision of Canal Zone laws—fixing status of offenses. Report. (To accompany H.R. 7519) [Washington, U.S. Govt. Print. Off., 1932] 37 p ([U.S.] 72d Congress, 1st session. Senate. Report no. 941)

J66
Serial no. 9488

Calendar no. 992.

Submitted by Mr. Schall. Ordered printed June 24 (calendar day, June 25), 1932.

The statutory common law era in private legal relations began formally in the zone with the first comprehensive Canal Zone code (of 1933–34), in the preparation of which there were innumerable hearings and reports in both chambers of the Congress. Only this one, and Senate report 943 (same call number and location symbol) are of any significant relevance to the subject of this bibliography. This report, particularly the first nine pages, contains some worthwhile historical information bearing on the uncertainty of the legal status of the zone in the early years under the Hay-Bunau Varilla Treaty. (2)

116

U.S. *Congress. House. Committee on Foreign Affairs.* Authorizing the execution of certain obligations under the treaties of 1903 and 1936 with Panama. Hearings before the Committee on Foreign Affairs, House of Representatives, Seventy-eighth Congress, first session, on H.J. Res. 14, a joint resolution authorizing the execution of certain obligations under the treaties of 1903 and 1936 with Panama, and other commitments. March 16, 1943. Statements of Mr. Philip W. Bonsal, Chief, Division of the American Republics, Department of State, [and] Mr. Green H. Hackworth, Legal Adviser, Department of State. Washington, U.S. Govt. Print. Off., 1943. 12 p.
                                        E183.8.P2U6
Sol Bloom, chairman.

Substantively, the matters under consideration were the return to Panama of sanitary responsibilities and water rates in the cities of Colón and Panama, the release to Panama of title to real estate in Colón owned by the Panama Railroad Company, and the granting by Panama of various sites throughout the republic. The time was the middle of World War II, and perhaps more important than the substance was the spirit of complete cooperation and friendliness then evidenced on both sides. There is some discussion of a legal point which has come up repeatedly and is very much involved in the current controversy; viz., the authority of Congress to dispose of public property under article IV, section 3, of the Constitution. (2)

117

U.S. *Congress. House. Committee on Merchant Marine and Fisheries.* Study of the operations of the Panama Canal Company and Canal Zone Government. Hearings before the Committee on Merchant Marine and Fisheries, House of Representatives, Eighty-fourth Congress, first session. March 29, 30, and 31, 1955. 104 p. illus., maps.   HE537.65 1955.A48

Herbert C. Bonner, chairman.

While this study is primarily concerned with commercial and engineering matters, it contains some tentative discussion of a sea-level canal, recognizing that the same would necessitate new treaty arrangements with Panama, and is possibly the first official document to associate the idea with the use of atomic power. A 1947 study, resulting from Public Law 280, 79th Congress, Dec. 28, 1945 (59 Stat. 663), suggested conversion of the existing canal to sea level, but the report failed to receive presidential approval and was transmitted to the Congress without recommendation and filed without congressional action thereon. (3)

118

U.S. *Congress. House. Committee on Foreign Affairs.* United States relations with Panama. Hearings before the Subcommittee on Inter-American Affairs of the Committee on Foreign Affairs, House of Representatives, Eighty-sixth Congress, second session. Washington, U.S. Govt. Print. Off., 1960. 107 p. diagr.   E183.8.P2U6 1960
Hearings held Jan. 12–Feb. 2, 1960.

These hearings illustrate the extent to which relations with Panama had deteriorated during the previous few years, culminating in the riots of 1959. Considerable discussion of symbolic issues, such as the flying of the flag, coupled with warnings by some witnesses against making any further concessions beyond those granted in the treaty of 1955. (1)

119

U.S. *Congress. House. Committee on Foreign Affairs.* Report on United States relations with Panama, by the Subcommittee on Inter-American Affairs of the Committee on Foreign Affairs, Eighty-sixth Congress, second session, pursuant to H. Res. 113, a resolution authorizing the Committee on Foreign Affairs to conduct thorough studies and investigations of all matters coming within the jurisdiction of such committee. Washington, U.S. Govt. Print. Off., 1960, 89 p. map. ([U.S.] 86th Congress, 2d session. House. Report no. 2218)   E183.8.P2U6 1960a
                                        Serial no. 12249
August 31, 1960.—Committed to the Committee of the Whole House on the State of the Union and ordered to be printed.

Much repetition, but a good summary of developments to date of publication and an interesting appendix showing concessions made to Panama in the treaties of 1936 and 1955. (2)

120

Flood, Daniel J. Isthmian Canal policy questions; Canal Zone-Panama Canal sovereignty, Panama Canal modernization, new canal. Selected addresses by Daniel J. Flood of Pennsylvania. Washington, U.S. Govt. Print. Off., 1966. 523, xiv p. illus., maps. ([U.S.] 89th Congress, 2d session. House. Doc. no. 474)
                                        HE537.65 1966.F56

Congressman Flood has been a keen student of Panama Canal affairs for many years, devoting more time and attention to the subject than any other one member of the House of Representatives. This document is a compilation made by him of selected addresses, as well as newspaper articles, letters, etc., covering the period from 1958 to 1966. Daniel Flood is the acknowledged leader in the House of the opposition to any weakening of U.S. treaty rights in the Canal Zone. (1)

121
Thurmond, Strom. Bibliography of Panama
Canal issues. Congressional record, [U.S.] 90th
Congress, 1st session, v. 113, July 10, 1967:
18,114–18,119.   J11.R5, v. 113

Sen. Strom Thurmond is the most militant
spokesman in the Senate for those members
who oppose any weakening of U.S. treaty rights
in the Canal Zone. In these pages of the
Congressional Record he has compiled a list of
works on the subject, in various categories, that
he considers worth reading, among which are
several that express a view distinctly contrary to
his own. (1)

122
——Panama Canal treaties. Congressional re-
cord, [U.S.] 90th Congress, 1st session, v. 113,
July 10, 1967: 18,119–18,121.   J11.R5, v. 113

Remarks of Senator Thurmond concerning
the abortive Panama Canal treaties of 1967 and
the part played by the *Chicago Tribune* in releas-
ing the texts thereof to the public (see entry
158). (2)

123
——Hand list of Panama Canal treaty statements. Congressional Record, [U.S.] 90th Congress, 1st session, v. 113, Aug. 15, 1967: 22,622.
                                        J11.R5, v. 113

Citation by Senator Thurmond, primarily for
the benefit of his Senate colleagues, of previous
statements which he has made on Panama Canal
matters and which have been printed in the
Congressional Record. (2)

124
U.S. *Congress. House. Committee on Merchant Ma-
rine and Fisheries. Subcommittee on Panama Canal.*
Report on the problems concerning the Panama
Canal. Washington, U.S. Govt. Print. Off., 1970.
96 p.   HE537.65.1970.A5
At head of title: 91st Congress, 2d session.
Committee print.

A relatively short, but excellent, updating to
1970 of the whole gamut of continuing problems, and attempts to reach solutions, arising
from the treaty relationships between the United
States and Panama and the perceived needs of
the United States in operating and planning for
the continued operation of the Panama Canal. A
good deal of attention is paid to the abortive
draft treaties of 1967: "In the view of the
subcommittee (subcommittee chairman and
ranking minority member), the assumptions underlying the 1967 drafts are not now valid if,
indeed, they ever were."
A particular criticism of the 1967 drafts is that
certain provisions therein disposing of federal

property took no account of the constitutional
responsibilities of the House of Representatives
in such a function (article IV, section 3, clause 2)
(see also entry 158). (1)

125
U.S. *Congress. House. Committee on Foreign Affairs.
Subcommittee on Inter-American Affairs.* Panama
Canal, 1971. Hearings, Ninety-second Congress,
first session on H. Res. 74, 154, 156, and other
resolutions to express the sense of the House of
Representatives that the United States maintain
its sovereignty and jurisdiction over the Panama
Canal Zone. September 22 and 23, 1971. Wash-
ington, U.S. Govt. Print. Off., 1971. 173. p
                               KF27.F646 1971

Statements for the record by a number of
representatives, led by Congressman Daniel
Flood, of opposition to treaty negotiations cur-
rently under way which would weaken the status
of the United States in the Panama Canal Zone
in any way. Also includes appendixes setting
forth the salient treaties now in effect between
the United States and Panama. One appendix
shows the concessions to Panama which have
already been made since the original Hay-Bunau
Varilla Treaty of 1903 (repetition of entry no.
119, p. 41 et seq.). (1)

126
U.S. *Congress. House. Committee on Merchant Ma-
rine and Fisheries. Subcommittee on Panama Canal.*
Panama Canal treaty negotiations. Hearings,
Ninety-second Congress. Washington, U.S. Govt.
Print. Off., 1972. 371 p.   KF27.M475 1971
    Hearings held Nov. 29, 1971–Aug. 10, 1972.
"Serial no. 92–30."
—— ——Addendum. Washington, U.S.
Govt. Print. Off., 1972 [i.e. 1973] 373–511 p.
illus.   KF27.M475 1971 Suppl
"Serial no. 92–30A."
Includes bibliographical references.

These hearings, presided over by Congressman Murphy, were held for the stated purpose
of clarifying the current status of Panama Canal
treaty negotiations and shedding "the light of
understanding where there is now the darkness
of uncertainty and speculation and fear." On the
whole, the hearings, including testimony from a
great many expert witnesses, accomplish that
purpose, and the document constitutes a vital
link in the recent record on the overall subject.
(1)

127
U.S. *Congress. House. Committee on Merchant Ma-
rine and Fisheries.* The Panama Canal and the
Panama Canal Company. *In its* Report on activi-

ties during the 92d Congress. [Washington, U.S. Govt. Print. Off., 1973?] (U.S. 92d Congress, 2d session. House. Report no. 92–1629) p. 19–44.

                                    Serial no. 12976–1B

This section of the cited committee report is introduced with the statement (p. 19): "By mandate of the full Merchant Marine and Fisheries Committee, the Panama Canal Subcommittee has the obligation and duty to guarantee the uninterrupted and efficient operation of the Panama Canal in the best interests of the United States."

Interpreting the mandate against the larger background of U.S.–Panamanian relations, and particularly the ongoing treaty negotiations, the subcommittee faces a number of sensitive issues with unflinching candor; such as the alleged failure of the Panamanian government to cooperate in the suppression of drug traffic, and increasingly strained relations between Panamanians and "Zonites" (p. 22–23):

It has been of increasing significance that the withdrawal from a position of amicable relationships to a position of isolation has characterized not only the Panamanians, but the Zonites as well. If such polarization is to be reversed and stability is ever to be achieved in the area, the natural cultural barriers that have been reenforced by ignorance, fear, and bigotry, abetted by a distorted press, must be eliminated on the part of all parties concerned. The establishment of an aggressive mass media campaign to remove these barriers is of utmost urgency.

The subcommittee says that the remaining key issues to be resolved are (p. 36):

(a) Retention by the United States of its undiluted sovereign rights, power and authority over the Canal Zone, which is the absolutely necessary protective frame of the Canal; and

(b) major modernization of the existing Canal within the present Canal Zone which means that we do not necessarily need a new treaty with Panama. (1)

128
U.S. *Congress. House. Committee on Foreign Affairs. Subcommittee on Inter-American Affairs.* United States relations with Panama. Hearing before the Subcommittee on Inter-American Affairs of the Committee on Foreign Affairs, House of Representatives, Ninety-Third Congress, first session. February 20, 1973. Washington, U.S. Govt. Print. Off., 1973. 53 p.   KF27.F646 1973b

A short but thought-provoking exploration of some of the hard problems that will have to be confronted and solved on the nuts-and-bolts level before a new treaty can actually be made to work. Consists mainly of a presentation by Robert A. Hurwitch, deputy assistant secretary for inter-American affairs, Department of State, and a speech by the Panamanian jurist Jorge Illueca which pulls no punches in articulating Panamanian expectations. (1)

129
——. United Nations Security Council Meeting on Panama. Hearing before the Subcommittees on Inter-American Affairs and International Organizations and Movements of the Committee on Foreign Affairs and the Subcommittee on Panama Canal of the Committee on Merchant Marine and Fisheries, House of Representatives, Ninety-third Congress, first session. April 3, 1973. Washington, U.S. Govt. Print. Off., 1973. 34 p.   HF27.F646 1973e

An explanation of the events leading up to and the reasons for the exercise by the United States of its third veto of a UN Security Council resolution (on Panama Canal treaty negotiations). (1)

130
U.S. *Congress. House. Committee on Merchant Marine and Fisheries. Subcommittee on Panama Canal.* Panama Canal briefings. Hearing, Ninety-third Congress, first session on briefings concerning treaty negotiations and current activities of the Panama Canal and Canal Zone. April 13, 1973. Washington, U.S. Govt. Print. Off., 1973. 78 p. illus.   KF27.M475 1973

"Serial no. 93–8."

Characterized as an oversight briefing, this hearing ranges rather widely over the general subject of treaty negotiations, revealing the concern of some members of the committee that Congress keep a close watch on proceedings and an admission by U.S. negotiators that the differences between the U.S. and Panamanian negotiating positions are still very great. One of the interesting points touched on briefly in the questioning is that the Canal Zone code would no longer apply to areas of the zone returned to the jurisdiction of Panama. (1)

131
——. Canal Zone policies and problems; hearings before the Subcommittee on Panama Canal of the House of Representatives, Ninety-Third Congress, second session, on general employment practices of the Panama Canal Company-Canal Zone Government and problems of the Latin American communities in the Canal Zone, July 26, 29, 1974. Washington, U.S. Govt. Print. Off., 1975. 215 p.   KF27.M475 1974a
"Serial no. 93–48."

These hearings were held in the administration building at Balboa Heights, Canal Zone. They cover a wide range of subjects—e.g., the school systems and equal employment opportunity—not bearing directly on the treaty controversy yet of such a nature, as the hearings implicitly and sometimes explicitly recognize, that they are bound to be affected by any basic changes in treaty status. The following brief excerpt (p. 5) from the opening statement of Gov. David S. Parker points up how extraordinarily complicated the situation in the zone really is:

> Not only are we involved in the same sort of rules and regulations which pertain to Federal agencies in the United States, but we also have a host of special circumstances imposed upon us by our treaty relationships with the Republic of Panama. These relationships do not have a parallel anywhere else in federal service.

Perhaps the unique importance of this document, however, is that it goes into a sensitive and vaguely identified area rarely referred to in official reports, viz., the interaction between ongoing U.S.-Panamanian treaty negotiations and the current state of mind of the non-American inhabitants of the zone who live in a more or less segregated society and whose condition of life will be affected by the outcome of such negotiations. (2)

132

——. GAO study of Canal Zone personnel policies. Hearings before the Subcommittee on Panama Canal of the Committee on Merchant Marine and Fisheries, House of Representatives, Ninety-fourth Congress, first session, on GAO Report no. B–114839 on study of various personnel policies of the Canal organizations and other Federal agencies in the Canal Zone. June 16, July 22, 1975. Washington, U.S. Govt. Print. Off., 1975. 397 p.   KF27.M475 1975
"Serial no. 94–8."
"GAO Report No. B–114839": p. 7–253.

This very lengthy and detailed study by the General Accounting Office is responsive to a formal request from the chairman of the Subcommittee on Panama Canal. It is not directly tied to the new treaty negotiations which, it is recognized, would introduce so many imponderables as to make such a study impossibly difficult. "Data presented in this report does not consider the effects of any new treaty being negotiated between the United States and the Republic of Panama." Nevertheless, in providing such a graphic description of the situation as is—in the basic human terms of conditions of employment, housing, tropical differential, discrimination, schooling, etc.—the report inevitably throws a great deal of light on matters which must be taken into account in assessing the consequences of changes which a new treaty relationship will bring about. (2)

133

Panama Canal. *In* U.S. *Congress. House. Committee on Appropriations. Subcommittee on the Dept. of Transportation and Related Agencies Appropriations.* Department of Transportation and related agencies appropriations for 1976. Hearings before a subcommittee of the Committee on Appropriations, House of Representatives, Ninety-fourth Congress, first session. pt. 4. Washington, U.S. Govt. Print. Off., 1975. p. 1–218. illus.

KF27.A667 1975

Though primarily concerned with rather technical fiscal matters, these hearings also touch on some of the same basic problems in human relations that were mentioned in entry 132—competition for housing and the criteria which should be used therefor, race, nationality, segregation, employment skills, wage scales, etc.—and, by inference, how they would be affected by a new treaty relationship eliminating the zone concept. (2)

D. U.S. Digests of International Law Practice

134

New Granada. *In* U.S. *Dept. of State.* Digest of the published opinions of the Attorneys General and of the leading decisions of the Federal courts, with reference to international law, treaties, and kindred subjects. Rev. ed. Washington, Govt. Print. Off., 1877. p. 249–250.   JX237.A48

Condensation of several opinions of attorneys general interpreting the Treaty of 1846 with New Granada, with particular emphasis on the crucial article 35. The whole of this work, prepared by John L. Cadwalader, consists of a single volume of less than three-hundred pages, with subjects arranged in alphabetical order rather than under chapter headings. It was the forerunner of the official digests of international law which began, strictly speaking, with the Wharton digest of 1886. (1)

135

Isthmus of Panama. *In* Wharton, Francis. A digest of the international law of the United States taken from documents issued by Presidents and Secretaries of State, and from decisions of Federal courts and opinions of Attorneys General. v. 3. Washington, Govt. Print. Off., 1886. p. 1–37.   JX237.W5, v. 3.

The excerpts herein reflect the growing interest of the United States in interoceanic transit, the possibility of a canal (the French canal project was already under way in 1881), and its effect on world trade and U.S. defense strategy. The most significant single excerpt is that from President Hayes's special message of March 8, 1880 (p. 3–4). (1)

136

Interoceanic communications. *In* Moore, John Bassett. A digest of international law as embodied in diplomatic discussions, treaties and other international agreements, international awards, the decisions of municipal courts, and the writings of jurists, and especially in documents, published and unpublished, issued by Presidents and Secretaries of State of the United States, and opinions of the Attorneys General, and the decisions of courts, Federal and state. v. 3. Washington, Govt. Print. Off., 1906. ([U.S.] 56th Congress, 2d session. House. Doc. 551) p. 1–262.
JX237.M7, v. 3

Coverage of the subject in this entry is so thorough and detailed, even including numerous useful side comments, as to constitute a narrativelike, patchwork diplomatic and international law history of the Panama Canal from 1835 to 1904. In addition to the evolution of relations with Colombia (exhaustive inquiry into application of the Treaty of 1846) and Panama, it also pays a great deal of attention to the Hay-Pauncefote Treaty and relations with Great Britain. The author, in his preface, points out a fact which makes this digest different in kind from all the other digests cited in this bibliography: "It will also be observed that, while the work bears the name and character of a digest, it also contains much that is of an expository nature, in a form suitable to a treatise." There is some repetition of material included in the previous Wharton digest of 1886. (1)

137

Panama Canal. *In* Hackworth, Green H. Digest of International Law. v. 2. Washington, U.S. Govt. Print. Off., 1942. [U.S. Dept. of State. Publication 1521] p. 772–814.   JX237.H3, v. 2

Material contained in Moore's digest is not duplicated, but judicious selection has been made of relevant documents from files accumulated since 1906. Principal topics are special status of Great Britain and Colombia with respect to tolls, problems of passage arising as a result of World War I, right of the United States to fortify the canal, abrogation of the Taft Agreement of 1904, and General Treaty of Friendship and Cooperation of March 2, 1936. In treating the Taft Agreement, this digest includes the vital and definitive statements of position of both Panama and the United States respecting basic questions of sovereignty in the zone under the Hay-Bunau Varilla Treaty. This correspondence is also published in *Foreign Relations of the United States*, v. 2, 1923, p. 638–75. (1)

138

Panama Canal. *In* Whiteman, Marjorie M. Digest of international law. v. 3. [Washington, U.S.

Dept. of State, 1964] (U.S. Dept. of State, Publication 7403) p. 1130–1256. JX237.W55, v. 3

Characterized by the author as the successor to Hackworth's digest, it does not duplicate material therein, but judicious selection has been made of relevant documents from files accumulated since 1942, as well as a few documents before 1942 which were not included in Hackworth. The most important single event (relative to the subject of this bibliography) which occurred during the twenty-year time span covered was the Treaty of Mutual Understanding and Cooperation of January 25, 1955. The Whiteman digest contains a helpful table showing the status (amendments, etc.), as of 1964, of all major conventions between the United States and Panama since 1903. The most meaningful single issue traced is that concerning the flying of the Panamanian flag in the zone, which eventually culminated in the traumatic riots of January 1964. (Information on subsequent investigation of the riots by the Inter-American Peace Committee may be found in Whiteman, v. 12, p. 811–14. See also entries 190 and 34.)

This digest makes greater use than any previous digest of unofficial legal writings, and wisely so as they provide more penetrating analyses than some of the official documents. Numerous judicial decisions are also cited. (1)

For the period from 1965 to 1972 there is a hiatus in digest coverage of the Panama Canal subject. The following significant items appeared in the *Department of State Bulletin.*

139

United States and Panama reestablish diplomatic relations. *In* U.S. *Dept. of State.* The Department of State bulletin, v. 50, Apr. 27, 1964: 655–656.
JX232.A33, v. 50

The essence of this item is the Joint Declaration of April 3, 1964, issued under the auspices of the Organization of American States, wherein the United States and Panama agreed to reestablish diplomatic relations and "to seek the prompt elimination of the causes of conflict between the two countries. . . ." Though the event occurred in 1964, it was not included in the Whiteman digest. (1)

140

U.S. plans new sea level canal and new treaty on existing canal. *In* U.S. *Dept. of State.* The Department of State bulletin, v. 52, Jan. 4, 1965: 5–6.
JX232.A33, v. 52

This is a statement by Pres. Lyndon B. Johnson issued in a White House press release on December 18, 1964, but not published officially until January 4, 1965. Two decisions are announced: to proceed with plans and preparations for a sea-level canal, and "to propose to the Government of Panama the negotiation of an entirely new treaty on the existing Panama Canal." The proposed new treaty would abrogate the 1903 treaty and amendments and would recognize the sovereignty of Panama, but would "retain the rights which are necessary for the effective operation and the protection of the canal and the administration of the areas that are necessary for these purposes." (1)

141
President reports on progress of negotiations with Panama. *In* U.S. *Dept. of State.* The Department of State bulletin, v. 53, Oct. 18, 1965: 624–625.   JX232.A33, v. 53

This is a statement of areas of agreement reached in the canal treaty negotiations with Panama. It was issued in a White House press release on September 24, 1965, and simultaneously released in Panama by President Robles. (1)

142
Department reviews Panama Canal treaty negotiations. *In* U.S. *Dept. of State.* The Department of State bulletin, v. 65, Dec. 27, 1971: 731–741.
                                      JX232.A33, v. 65

Statements made before the Subcommittee on the Panama Canal of the House Committee on Merchant Marine and Fisheries on November 29 by John C. Mundt, special representative of the United States for Panama treaty negotiations; Robert A. Hurwitch, deputy assistant secretary for Inter-American affairs; and Carl F. Salans, deputy legal adviser of the Department of State. General review of history of treaty negotiations and U.S.-Panamanian relations. Examination of constitutional law questions which would be involved in the transfer to Panamanian jurisdiction of territory and property now in the zone. (1)

143
A modern treaty for the Panama Canal. *In* U.S. *Dept. of State.* The Department of State bulletin, v. 66, June 12, 1972: 818–822.   JX232.A33, v. 66

Address made on May 12 by Ambas. David H. Ward, special representative of the United States for Panama Canal treaty negotiations. Argument is made that both Panamanian aspirations and U.S. interests would be served by a new treaty relationship which takes account of changed conditions since 1903. (1)

[Compiler's note: Beginning in 1973 the general and more comprehensive digests, covering lengthy time spans, which had been published at irregular intervals since 1877, were abandoned in favor of a new type of digest published annually. The new digest is limited to events of the calendar year.]

144
Canals: The Panama Canal. *In* Rovine, Arthur W. Digest of United States practice in international law. 1973. [Washington, 1974] (U.S. Dept. of State. Publication 8756) p. 273–276.
                                           JX21.R68

This item deals solely with the draft resolution on the Panama Canal introduced on March 21, 1973, at the UN Security Council meeting in Panama. The draft resolution was not adopted owing to exercise of the veto power by the United States. For the complete text of the resolution, as well as a report on the Security Council meeting, see *United Nations Security Council Meeting in Panama* (entry 129). (1)

145
Canals: Panama Canal. *In* Rovine, Arthur W. Digest of United States practice in international law. 1974. [Washington, 1975] (U.S. Dept. of State. Publication 8809) p. 355–356.   JX21.R68

Referring to the Joint Declaration of April 3, 1964 (see entry 139), this is a joint statement issued on February 7, 1974, by Secretary of State Henry A. Kissinger and Juan Antonio Tack, minister of foreign affairs of the Republic of Panama, wherein it is agreed that the 1903 treaty will be abrogated by the conclusion of a new treaty and that the "Panamanian territory in which the canal is situated shall be returned to the jurisdiction of the Republic of Panama." It further provides that the operation of the canal itself will eventually be turned over to Panama (see also entry 140). This Kissinger-Tack joint statement was previously published in volume 70 of *Department of State Bulletin* 184. (1)

146
The Panama Canal negotiations: popular myths and political realities. *In* U.S. *Dept. of State.* The Department of State bulletin, v. 73, Dec. 22, 1975: 881–885.   JX232.A33, v. 73

Address made on December 2, 1975, by Ambassador-at-Large Ellsworth Bunker, chief U.S. negotiator for the Panama Canal treaty, before the World Affairs Council at Los Angeles, California.
A concise and forceful statement of the case for a new Panama Canal treaty, including a summary of agreements reached in principle and issues remaining to be resolved as of the date of the address. As Ambassador Bunker says: "The real choice before us is not between the existing treaty and a new one but, rather, between a new treaty and what will happen if we should fail to achieve a new treaty." (1)

E. Treaties (and Certain International Agreements Other Than Treaties)

The official version of all treaties prior to January 1, 1950, was published in the *United States Statutes at Large*. Since January 1, 1950, the official version has been published in *United States Treaties and Other International Agreements* in accordance with the Act of September 23, 1950, chap. 1001, no. 2, 64 Stat. 979.

147
U.S. *Treaties, etc., 1845–1849 (Polk)*. Treaty with New Granada, Dec. 12, 1846. Treaty with New Granada. A general treaty of peace, amity, navigation, and commerce between the United States of America and the Republic of New Granada. *In* U.S. *Laws, statutes, etc*. The United States statutes at large and treaties of the United States of America. v. 9. Boston, Little and Brown, 1851. p. 881–901.   LL
Proclamation made June 12, 1848.

In English and Spanish.

This is the germinal treaty which marked the beginning of official U.S. involvement in interoceanic transit across the Isthmus of Panama, leading eventually to the existing Panama Canal. It would have been a routine commercial treaty except for article XXXV in which fateful commitments were made by both parties. The government of New Granada (now Colombia) guaranteed to the government of the United States a right of transit across the isthmus by whatever mode of communication may be constructed, and the government of the United States guaranteed to protect the neutrality and sovereignty of New Granada on the isthmus. It was the first radical break with Washington's advice to "steer clear of permanent Alliances with any portion of the foreign world." (1)

148
U.S. *Treaties, etc., 1849–1850 (Taylor)*. Treaty with Great Britain, April 19, 1850. [Clayton-Bulwer Treaty] Convention between the United States of America and Her Britannic Majesty. *In* U.S. *Laws, statutes, etc*. The United States statutes at large and treaties of the United States of America. v. 9. Boston, Little and Brown, 1851. p. 995–998.   LL
Proclamation made July 4, 1850.

In a breach of the Monroe Doctrine, the U.S. government in this treaty agreed never to obtain or maintain for itself exclusive control over any ship canal which might be constructed between the Atlantic and Pacific oceans. This was later seen to have been a serious diplomatic blunder which hindered American planning for a canal until abrogated by the Hay-Pauncefote Treaty of 1901. (See also entry 92.) (1)

149
Exhibit E: Contracts between the Republic of New Granada and the Panama Railroad Company, made in 1850 and 1867, and modified in 1876, 1880, and 1891. *In* Report of Joseph L. Bristow, Special Panama Railroad Commissioner to the Secretary of War, June 24, 1905. Published by Office of Administration, Isthmian Canal Affairs. Washington, Govt. Print. Off., 1906. ([U.S.] 59th Congress, 1st session. Senate. Doc. no. 429) p. 209–237.   J66
Serial no. 4919

This agreement with a private New York corporation to build a railroad across the isthmus was, in effect, the beginning of the implementation of the Treaty of 1846 (entry 147). From its inception the Panama Railroad has been inextricably entangled with the affairs of the Panama Canal. This contract, rewritten as an independent document in April 1850, had its antecedents in an earlier transisthmian railroad concession to a French company which was forfeited and the text of which appears in House Report 26, "Railroad Across the Isthmus of Panama, January 16, 1849" (30th Congress, 2d session). (1)

150
Exhibit C: Concession of 1878 and extensions. Wyse Concession, March 20, 1878. Contract for the construction of an interoceanic canal across Colombian territory. *In* U.S. *Dept. of Justice*. Official opinions of the Attorneys General of the United States, advising the President and heads of departments in relation to their official duties, and expounding the Constitution, treaties with foreign governments and with Indian tribes, and the public laws of the country. v. 24. Edited by John L. Lott and James A. Finch. Washington, Govt. Print. Off., 1903. ([U.S.] 57th Congress, 2d session. House. Doc. no. 493) p. 337–354. LL

The so-called Wyse Concession of March 20, 1878, which was the legal foundation for the French canal-building project, required in terms the prior acquiescence of the Panama Railroad Company (see entry 149) because of rights granted to that company in the contract of 1850. Acquiescence was obtained by the device of buying up nearly all the stock of that company. The property of the French canal company, including the railroad, was, in turn, bought up by the U.S. government pursuant to the Spooner Act of June 28, 1902 (32 Stat. 481). This document (Wyse Concession) is also published in *Panama Canal Title* (entry 160). (1)

151

U.S. *Treaties, etc., 1901–1909 (Roosevelt)*. Treaty between the United States and Great Britain, to facilitate the construction of a ship canal, November 18, 1901. [Hay-Pauncefote Treaty] *In* U.S. *Laws, statutes, etc.* The statutes at large of the United States of America. v. 32, pt. 2. Private laws, concurrent resolutions, treaties, and proclamations. Washington, Govt. Print. Off., 1903. p. 1903–1905.

Proclamation made February 22, 1902.   LL

This treaty specifically superseded the Clayton-Bulwer Treaty (entry 148) and left the U.S. government free to construct and control the canal so far as Great Britain was concerned. The first treaty draft intended to accomplish that objective was signed by Secretary of State John Hay and British Ambassador Lord Pauncefote on February 5, 1900, but was never ratified primarily because the Senate objected to clauses forbidding fortification of the canal or closing it in time of war. These provisions were omitted from the approved treaty. The text of the unperfected first treaty appears in Senate document 160, 56th Congress, 1st session. (1)

152

Hay-Herran Treaty. *In* U.S. *Dept. of State*. Diplomatic history of the Panama Canal. Correspondence relating to the negotiation and application of certain treaties on the subject of the construction of an interoceanic canal and accompanying papers. Washington, Govt. Print. Off., 1914. ([U.S.] 63rd Congress, 2d session. Senate. Doc. 474) p. 277–288.   JX1398.5.A5 1914

Although this draft treaty was never perfected, it is important historically because its rejection by the Colombian Senate provided much of the impetus for the Panamanian Revolution of November 1903 and for purposes of comparison with the Hay-Bunau Varilla Treaty (entry 153) which quickly followed. The text of the unperfected draft treaty also appears in *The Fight for the Panama Route* (entry 49), *An Historical Reappraisal of the Hay-Herran Treaty* (entry 45), and other places. (1)

153

U.S. *Treaties, etc., 1901–1909 (Roosevelt)*. Convention between the United States and the Republic of Panama for the construction of a ship canal to connect the waters of the Atlantic and Pacific Oceans, November 18, 1903. [Hay-Bunau Varilla Treaty] *In* U.S. *Laws, Statutes, etc.* The statutes at large of the United States of America. v. 33, pt. 2. Private laws, concurrent resolutions, treaties, and proclamations. Washington, Govt. Print. Off., 1905. p. 2234–2241.   LL

Proclamation made February 26, 1904.

Although amended several times—most nota-

bly in 1936 (entry 155) and 1955 (entry 157)—this is still the operative treaty under which the United States maintains control of the Canal Zone and the Panama Canal. In short, this document is what the controversy is all about. Its most objectionable features from the Panamanian point of view remain intact, e.g., the granting to the United States of the power to exercise "sovereignty" over the zone and the "perpetuity" clause. The text of this treaty also appears in *Treaties and Other International Agreements of the United States of America 1776–1949*, v. 10 (Dept. of State Publication 8642), p. 663–72; and Senate Document 474, 63d Congress, 2d session, *Diplomatic History of the Panama Canal*, p. 295–303, and other places. (1)

154

Treaty: Colombia. April 6, 1914. Treaty between the United States and Colombia for the settlement of differences. [Thomson-Urrutia Treaty] Signed at Bogotá, April 6, 1914; ratification advised by the Senate with amendments, April 20, 1921; ratified by the President, January 11, 1922; ratified by Colombia, March 1, 1922; ratifications exchanged at Bogotá, March 1, 1922; proclaimed March 30, 1922. *In* U.S. *Laws, statutes, etc.* United States at large, containing the laws and concurrent resolutions . . . and reorganization plan, amendment to the Constitution, and proclamations. v. 42, pt. 2. Washington, Govt. Print. Off., 1923. p. 2122–2127.   LL

In English and Spanish.

This treaty finally ended the long dispute with Colombia over the U.S. role in the Panamanian Revolution of November 1903 and the legality of the Hay-Bunau Varilla Treaty. Colombia recognized the fait accompli of Panamanian independence in exchange for the payment of $25 million and certain special privileges in the use of the canal. Though signed in 1914, it was not proclaimed until 1922 after the Senate deleted an article expressing "sincere regret" that anything had occurred to mar relations between the two countries. The main reason that ratification was delayed for so long was that many influential Americans, led by ex-President Theodore Roosevelt (see entry 255), were bitterly opposed to any admission, even by inference, that Colombia was entitled to redress for American actions which Colombia held to be in violation of the Treaty of 1846. (1)

155

U.S. *Treaties, etc., 1939–1945 (Franklin D. Roosevelt)*. General treaty of friendship and cooperation between the United States of America and Panama, March 2, 1936. (Sometimes called the Hull-Alfaro Treaty) *In* U.S. *Laws, statutes, etc.* United States statutes at large. v. 53, pt. 3.

Private laws, concurrent resolutions, treaties, international agreements other than treaties, and proclamations. Washington, U.S. Govt. Print. Off., 1939. p. 1807–1873.   LL

Proclamation made July 27, 1939.

Also published separately as no. 945 in the Treaty Series.

In English and Spanish.

The most significant provisions of this treaty, in their long-range effect on the continuing and sensitive issue of sovereignty, are found in articles I, II, and VI. The first paragraph of article I abrogates, in effect, article I of the Hay-Bunau Varilla Treaty wherein the United States guaranteed to maintain the independence of Panama, thus making Panama, in the Panamanian view, appear as a dependency of the United States. Article II limits the rights granted the United States in article II of the Hay-Bunau Varilla Treaty to acquire additional lands and waters outside the zone. Article VI abrogates the third paragraph of article VII of the Hay-Bunau Varilla Treaty which gave the United States the right to intervene, if necessary to maintain order, in certain territories of the republic including the two largest cities.

This treaty was followed by several exchanges of notes and supplementary conventions, which are explained in entry 137, p. 807–14. (1)

156
U.S. *Treaties, etc., 1933–1945 (Franklin D. Roosevelt).* General relations. Agreements between the United States of America and Panama, effected by exchange of notes signed at Washington May 18, 1942. Washington, U.S. Govt. Print. Off., 1945. 10 p. ([U.S. Dept. of State. Publication 2431] Executive agreement series 452)

JX1428.P2U5 1942b

Also published in *United States Statutes at Large,* v. 59, pt. 2, p. 1289–1297.

In this executive agreement the U.S. government acceded to a number of requests which the Republic of Panama had put forward for certain benefits or amelioration of certain perceived problems arising from the existence of the canal and the zone in the middle of the republic; such as, the United States promised to transfer to Panama the water and sewer systems installed by the United States in the cities of Panama and Colón, convey to Panama certain real estate holdings of the Panama Railroad, bear all the cost of the highway between Chorrera and Río Hato, build a bridge over or a tunnel under the canal in order to facilitate transit, cooperate with the immigration policies of Panama, and cooperate in preventing smuggling from the zone into the republic.

On the same date a separate executive agreement made available to the United States numerous sites in the republic needed for military purposes in connection with World War II. (1)

157
Panama. Mutual understanding and cooperation. Treaty, with memorandum of understandings reached, signed at Panama January 25, 1955. (Sometimes called the Eisenhower-Remon Treaty) *In* U.S. *Treaties, etc.* United States treaties and other international agreements. v. 6, pt. 2, 1955. [Washington, U.S. Govt. Print. Off., 1956] p. 2273–2367.   JX231.A34

U.S. Dept. of State. Treaties and other international acts series, 3297

Proclamation made August 26, 1955.

In English and Spanish.

Article I raises the annuity payable to the Republic of Panama from $430,000 to $1,930,000. Article II gives the republic the right to impose an income tax on its own citizens working in the zone, thus modifying article X of the Hay-Bunau Varilla Treaty. Article III abrogates article V of the Hay-Bunau Varilla Treaty which gave the United States a monopoly in perpetuity for the construction and operation of any canal or railroad across the territory of the republic, and likewise abrogates a similar monopoly of the Panama Railroad with respect to roads. The bulk of the treaty is taken up with territorial and boundary adjustments. It also had significant effects, however, on personnel policies, especially as related to conditions of employment of non-U.S. citizens. (1)

158
Appendix IV. Text of proposed treaty on canal; U.S., Panama would create operating unit. Appendix V. Treaty between the Republic of Panama and the United States of America concerning a sea level canal connecting the Atlantic and Pacific Oceans. Appendix VI. Treaty on the defense of the Panama Canal and of its neutrality, June 21, 1967. *In* U.S. *Congress. House. Committee on Merchant Marine and Fisheries. Subcommittee on Panama Canal.* Report on the problems concerning the Panama Canal. Washington, U.S. Govt. Print. Off., 1970. p. 38–81.

HE537.65.1970.A5

At head of title: 91st Congress, 2d session. Committee print.

Pursuant to the statement of President Johnson on December 18, 1964 (entry 140), the United States entered into negotiations with Panama in 1965 culminating in 1967 in these three separate but interdependent treaty drafts dealing with, respectively, the return to Panamanian control of most of the area of the zone and the creation of a new joint administration of the existing canal (appendix IV), the building of a sea-level canal (appendix V), and status of forces and use of facilities for military purposes (appendix VI). The drafts were never submitted to the ratification process in either country and were never released to the public by the Department of State. Copies were obtained in Panama by, and published in, the *Chicago Tribune* and subsequently reprinted in the *Congressional Record* of July 17, 21, and 27, 1967, then further reprinted together in this subcommittee report. Though the subcommittee report (p. 4) only says that they are "purported to be official texts," the texts are, in fact, accurate. The importance of these draft treaties, though unperfected and strongly opposed in both countries, is emphasized in entry 124, p. 5, and entry 162, p. 2 and p. 11–12. (1)

F. Opinions of Attorneys General

159
The Isthmus of Panama. *In* U.S. *Dept. of Justice.* Official opinions of the Attorneys General of the United States, advising the President and heads of departments in relation to their official duties. v. 11, Washington, W. H. & O. H. Morrison, 1869. p. 391–393.   LL

The gist of this opinion is that article 35 of the Treaty of 1846 with New Granada (later Colombia) does not obligate the United States to protect the Isthmus of Panama against internal insurrection, but only against invasion by a foreign power. It is limited to that point and does not enter into the eventuality, as actually happened in 1903, that the United States might obstruct the movement of Colombian troops across the isthmus. Nevertheless, it was a significant opinion with far-reaching import and was still being cited many years later in legal treatises, such as entries 193 and 196. (1)

160
U.S. *Dept. of Justice.* Panama Canal title. Opinion of the Attorney General upon the title proposed to be given by the New Panama Canal Company to the United States. Washington, Govt. Print. Off., 1902. 335 p.   TC774.U43 1902
                                                                                    LL

Section 4 of the Spooner Act of June 28, 1902 (32 Stat. 481), provided that the president must obtain a satisfactory title to the property of the (French-owned) New Panama Canal Company before proceeding with the construction of a canal across the Isthmus of Panama. In this exhaustive opinion, pursuant to that requirement, the attorney general concluded that there was no legal impediment to the passage of a

valid and unencumbered title. The effect, if any, of the later, and unforeseen, separation of Panama from Colombia is, of course, not considered in the opinion. (This document is also published in v. 24, *Attorneys General Opinions,* p. 144.) (1)

161
Tariff Act of 1909: Canal Zone. *In* U.S. *Dept. of Justice.* Official opinions of the Attorneys General of the United States, advising the President and heads of departments in relation to their official duties. v. 27. Washington, Govt. Print. Off., 1909. p. 594–597.   LL

The tariff act approved August 5, 1909 (36 Stat. 11), provided for the rates of duty to be paid upon articles "imported from any foreign country into the United States or into any of its possessions. . . ." The question presented was whether the Canal Zone is "one of its possessions." Quoting from the syllabus of the opinion:

The Canal Zone is not one of the possessions of the United States within the meaning of the tariff act of 1909, but rather a place subject to the use, occupation, and control of the United States for the purpose of constructing and maintaining a ship canal connecting the waters of the Atlantic and Pacific oceans. (2)

G. Sea Level Canal Study

162
U.S. *Atlantic-Pacific Interoceanic Canal Study Commission.* Interoceanic canal studies, 1970. [Washington, 1970] 1 v. (various pagings) illus., maps (part col.).   TC773.U23
Includes Annexes 1–5.

Public Law 88–609 of September 22, 1964, 88th Congress (78 Stat. 990)—three months before President Johnson's statement on December 18, 1964, of intention to negotiate a new treaty with Panama on the existing canal and to investigate the feasibility of a sea-level canal—authorized the president to appoint a commission to make a comprehensive study of all aspects of a possible sea-level canal connecting the Atlantic and Pacific oceans. This volume is the final report of that commission. The study commenced in 1965 and ran concurrently for the first two years with the treaty negotiations which culminated in the drafts of 1967. Though Robert B. Anderson was both chairman of the commission and principal U.S. treaty negotiator, the two activities were completely separate, at least in theory. "However," as this final report says, "the Commission has been mindful of relevant provisions of the draft treaties in its consideration of possible future treaty arrangements that would bear upon the feasibility of a sea level canal in Panama."

In its covering letter to the president the commission recommends that "the United States negotiate with Panama a treaty that provides for a unified canal system, comprising both the existing canal and a sea level canal on Route 10 [outside the zone about ten miles west of the existing canal], to be operated and defended under the effective control of the United States with participation by Panama." For purposes of this bibliography, attention is directed to annex I, "Study of Foreign Policy Considerations," p. I-iii–I-59. (1)

H. Canal Zone Supreme Court

163

Canal Zone. *Supreme Court.* Canal Zone Supreme Court reports. Cases adjudged in the Supreme Court of the Canal Zone from July term, 1905, to [June 1914] Ancon, Isthmian Canal Commission Press, 1909–15, 2 v. (Canal Zone reports, v. 1–2)   LL

Imprint for v. 2: Mount Hope, C.Z., Panama Canal Press.

Reporters: v. 1, Walter Emery.—v. 2, T. C. Hinckley and Stevens Ganson.

The Canal Zone Supreme Court was constituted as of June 1, 1905, and expired on June 30, 1914. It was not only a territorial court of last resort, but a court of last resort for all purposes as no provision was made for appeal to any higher court in the United States. Two attempts to appeal to the U.S. Supreme Court both failed on the threshold question of jurisdiction. Several of the cases reported involved interpretation of the treaty relationships between the United States and Panama. (1)

164

U.S. *District Court. Canal Zone.* Cases adjudged in the District Court for the Canal Zone from May 1, 1914, to January 1, 1926. Mount Hope, C.Z., Panama Canal Press, 1927. 651 p. (Canal Zone reports, v. 3)   LL

The Panama Canal Act of 1912 established a U.S. District Court for the Canal Zone to replace the defunct Canal Zone Supreme Court. It was incorporated into the federal system but its decisions for the period covered by this volume were not otherwise reported. Several of the cases involved interpretation of the treaty relationships between the United States and Panama, and a few were appealed to and decided by the U.S. Supreme Court on grounds directly or indirectly involving such relationships. (1)

I. Decisions of the Supreme Court of the United States

165

In the matter of the application of Oli Nifou for a writ of habeas corpus [198 U.S. 581]. *In* U.S. *Supreme Court.* Records and briefs in United States cases decided by the Supreme Court of the United States, during the October term, 1904. Washington, Judd & Detweiler [1904?] 6 pts.

Contents: Application for original writs of habeas corpus and certiorari. 14 p.—Brief and argument in favor of the application for the writ of habeas corpus. 23 p.—Brief for the United States on motion for leave to file. 32 p.—Addendum to brief for United States. 2 p.—Answer to objections raised by the United States for leave to file. 20 p.—Petition to reconsider the ruling by which the application for original writs of habeas corpus and certiorari was denied. 6 p.
                                                LL

Badly neglected by historians, this was the first case from the Canal Zone to reach the Supreme Court of the United States. In a per curiam decision without opinion the court refused to hear it on the merits, presumably for lack of jurisdiction as Congress had made no provision for appeal from the highest court of the Canal Zone. Consequently, the fundamental questions respecting the nature and juridical basis of U.S. jurisdiction in the Canal Zone under the treaty, as raised in the records and briefs, were never reached. They did not go away, however, but were merely postponed, and continue, in large measure, to be postponed to the present day. The arguments and rebuttals in the records and briefs in this abortive case of 1904 are still timely. (For more on this case, see entry 12a, p. 81–82.) (1)

166

Wilson v. Shaw, Secretary of the Treasury. Appeal from the Court of Appeals of the District of Columbia. *In* U.S. *Supreme Court.* United States reports. v. 204. Cases adjudged in the Supreme Court at October term, 1906. New York, Banks Law Pub. Co., 1907. p. 24–35. LL

This suit was an attempt by a taxpayer to invoke the aid of the courts to stop all expenditure of public monies for the purpose of constructing the Panama Canal on the grounds that whatever title the United States has was not acquired, in accordance with the act of June 28, 1902 (Spooner Act), by treaty with Colombia. As the court said: "The magnitude of the plaintiff's demand is somewhat startling." Nevertheless, although upholding "the action of the Executive in regard thereto" and finding that "the concurrent action of Congress and the Executive in this respect is conclusive upon the courts" it is interesting that the court recognized enough weight in the plaintiff's agrument to take the suit seriously and not dismiss it out of hand. This decision became the precedent for disposing of all subsequent attempts to challenge the "title" of the United States to the Canal Zone. (1)

167

Adolphus Coulson, plaintiff in error, v. the Government of the Canal Zone [212 U.S. 553] *In* U.S. *Supreme Court*. Records and briefs in United States cases decided by the Supreme Court of the United States, during the October term, 1907–[8. Washington, 1907–8?] 6 pts.   LL

Contents: Transcript of record. 70 p.—Motions to dismiss or affirm, and brief in support thereof. 12 p.—Brief in opposition to motion to dismiss or affirm. 16 p.—Brief in opposition to motion to dismiss or affirm. 30 p.—Petition for writ of habeas corpus and writ of certiorari with motion for leave to file same. 12 p.—Brief in opposition, filed by leave of court. 13 p.

This was the second and last case to reach the Supreme Court from the Canal Zone during the period of temporary government (prior to the reorganization effected by the Panama Canal Act of 1912). Like the other (Oli Nifou, entry 165), it was rejected by the court on the threshold ground of jurisdiction. Plaintiff in error, who had been convicted in a capital case without trial by jury, alleged that his constitutional rights had thereby been violated. The court in effect, by refusing to hear the case, held, consistent with the Insular cases, that the constitution did not extend to the Canal Zone. (1)

168

No. 127. Gideon Dixon et al., Appellants, v. George W. Goethals, et al. Appeal from the United States Circuit Court of Appeals for the Fifth Circuit (221 Fed. 1021). *In* U.S. *Supreme Court*. United States reports. v. 242. Cases adjudged in the Supreme Court at October term, 1916. New York, Banks Law Pub. Co., 1917. p. 616.   LL

Both the Circuit Court of Appeals and the Supreme Court affirmed the decision of the District Court, Canal Zone (v. 3 *Canal Zone Reports*, p. 23) to the effect that provisions in the Hay-Bunau Varilla Treaty for the expropriation of land in the Canal Zone took precedence over conflicting provisions in the Constitution of Panama. Quoting the syllabus of the District Court decision: "Where a government, by treaty, parts with sovereignty over a part of its domain, the new sovereign may legislate with respect

thereto without regard to constitutional provisions of the granting sovereign." (1)

169

Panama Railroad Company v. Bosse. Error to the Circuit Court of Appeals for the Fifth Circuit. *In* U.S. *Supreme Court*. United States reports. v. 249. Cases adjudged in the Supreme Court at October term, 1918. New York, The Banks Law Publishing Co., 1919. p. 41.   LL

Shortly after the United States took control of the zone, Pres. Theodore Roosevelt decreed in an executive order that "the laws of the land, with which the inhabitants are familiar" would remain in force. This was construed to keep in force the Civil Code of the Republic of Panama (until 1933), but a tendency immediately set in to construe the code in accordance with common law principles, and thus virtually to replace the former civil law principles for all practical purposes. The Bosse decision marked the culmination of that trend, which Mr. Justice Holmes justified by taking express notice of the fact that the nature of the population had completely changed since all privately owned land in the zone was expropriated and hence, by inference, the reasoning behind the executive order was no longer valid (see also entry 12a, p. 109–110). If all or part of the zone is returned to the jurisdiction of Panama under a new treaty, the matter of applying "laws . . . with which the inhabitants are familiar" will again become relevant. (2).

170

Panama Railroad Company v. Toppin. Error to the Circuit Court of Appeals for the Fifth Circuit. *In* U.S. *Supreme Court*. United States reports. v. 252. Cases adjudged in the Supreme Court at October term, 1919. New York, The Banks Law Publishing Co., 1920. p. 308.   LL

The main contentions of the plaintiff in error (Panama Railroad Company) were the same as in Bosse (entry 169); that the trial court erred in holding applicable the common law rules of respondeat superior and recovery for physical pain, the principal difference being that Bosse had occurred in the Canal Zone whereas Toppin occurred in the Republic of Panama. Both parties pleaded the law of Panama, which, formally at least, was in effect in both jurisdictions, but Justice Brandeis construed it to reach a common law result. The Bosse decision was reinforced and extended. (2)

171

Domingo Díaz A., et al. v. Patterson. Appeal from the Circuit Court of Appeals for the Fifth Circuit. *In* U.S. *Supreme Court*. United States reports. v. 263. Cases adjudged in the Supreme

Court at October term, 1923. Washington, Govt. Print. Off., 1924. p. 399.   LL

This decision moved the reception of the American common law in the Canal Zone a substantial step further by making explicit what had been left somewhat to inference in Bosse (entry 169), and by distinguishing Puerto Rico, where the Spanish civil law was still applicable, from the Canal Zone, where it clearly was not, regardless of the civil code still formally in effect. Quoting from the court's decision: "Under existing conditions, the occasions when the Executive Order referred to [entry 75, Executive Order of May 9, 1904] can be invoked must be few, and these few must continue to grow fewer. . . . But the considerations that have been urged for following local decisions in places like Puerto Rico having their own peculiar system, do not apply in the same degree to a code that in its present application governs a predominantly American population and derives its force from Congress and the President." (2)

172

McConaughey, for himself and others, employees of the Panama Canal and of the Panama Railroad Company, v. Morrow, Governor of the Panama Canal, et al. Appeal from the Circuit Court of Appeals for the Fifth Circuit. *In* U.S. *Supreme Court.* United States reports. v. 263. Cases adjudged in the Supreme Court at October term, 1923. Washington, Govt. Print. Off., 1924. p. 39.   LL

This suit, in part somewhat reminiscent of Oli Nifou (entry 165), attacked the very foundation of the civil government in the Canal Zone, and hence is a vital case in domestic law as it legitimized the legislation of the Isthmian Canal Commission by some very convoluted reasoning which reached a desired practical result in the immediate case while establishing a more important principle at variance therewith. This entry is placed in category 3 in this bibliography because it is only tenuously linked to the Hay-Bunau Varilla Treaty by reaching for the inferential question (now perhaps academic) of whether the establishment of any civil government in the zone can be supported by the language of the treaty. (3)

173

Panama Railroad Company v. Rock. Error to the Circuit Court of Appeals for the Fifth Circuit. *In* U.S. *Supreme Court.* United States reports. v. 266. Cases adjudged in the Supreme Court at October term, 1924. Washington, Govt. Print. Off., 1925. p. 209.   LL

This decision is in the main line of the decisions in entries 169, 170, and 171, but involves a new principle, that of the common

law rule on wrongful death, which appeared to be in conflict with an article of the civil code. Quoting from the syllabus of the court's decision:

> The Executive Order [of May 9, 1904] and the Act of 1912 [Panama Canal Act], having continued in force in the Canal Zone the laws of the land "with which the inhabitants are familiar," the population there having immediately become largely American, and the local courts having adopted common law principles in construing statutes, the article should be construed in accordance with the common law, as not granting a private cause of action for death by negligence.

Mr. Justice Holmes strongly dissented on the grounds that the common law rule itself had already been so diluted by the statutory trend in the United States as to be too weak to overcome the plain meaning of the civil code provision which would have allowed recovery. (2)

174

Luckenbach Steamship Company v. United States. Certiorari to the Court of Claims. *In* U.S. *Supreme Court.* United States reports. v. 280. Cases adjudged in the Supreme Court at October term, 1929. Washington, Govt. Print. Off., 1930. p. 173.   LL

The steamship company claimed that, in delivering mail to the Canal Zone, it was entitled to the higher rates provided by law for delivery to a "foreign" port. The brief for the United States, defendant, relying in part on Wilson v. Shaw (entry 166), contended that Canal Zone ports were ports of the United States. The court held, however, to the contrary. Quoting from the syllabus of the court's decision: "Ports in the Canal Zone are to be regarded as foreign ports within the meaning of Rev. Stats. # 4009, U.S. Code, Title 39, # 654, dealing with the compensation allowable for transportation of mail, by United States ships, between the United States and 'any foreign port.' " (1)

175

Vermilya-Brown Co., Inc. et al. v. Connell et al. Certiorari to the United States Court of Appeals for the Second Circuit. *In* U.S. *Supreme Court.* United States reports. v. 335. Cases adjudged in the Supreme Court at October term, 1948. Washington, Govt. Print. Off., 1949. p. 377.

LL

This case arose over the applicability of the Fair Labor Standards Act in a military area in Bermuda leased from Great Britain for ninety-nine years. In delivering the opinion of the court, however, Mr. Justice Reed, in obiter dicta, makes reference to the Canal Zone as "admittedly territory over which we do not have sovereignty." On the other hand, the decision seems to approve the inclusion of the Canal Zone within the meaning of "possession" (see also entry 161) because it is "an area vital to our national life." The decision also, in footnote 12, vividly illustrates the inconsistency with which Congress has dealt with the question of extending, or not extending, general legislation to the Canal Zone. (2)

J. Decisions of the U.S. District Court for the Canal Zone

176
Playa de Flor Land & Improvement Co. v. United States, Civ. no. 969. District Court, D. Canal Zone, Div. Cristobal, March 20, 1945. Federal supplement; cases argued and determined in the District Courts of the United States and the Court of Claims, v. 70, 1947: 281–376.   LL

Reduced to its bare bones, this entry was simply an action by plaintiff to fix just compensation for lands taken by executive order for purposes connected with the Panama Canal. However, as Judge Bunk Gardner observed in his extraordinarily scholarly and exhaustive opinion, it was "an unusual and unprecedented case" which had lingered in the courts for thirty-seven years before this decision, which took several years to write, finally disposed of it. It is placed in category 3 because it cannot be said to have much immediate relevance to the current treaty controversy (though, see sections 35 and 51 of the syllabus), but it will tell you everything you always wanted to know about land titles in the zone, including the effect thereon of the conflict of civil and common law and of the Hay-Bunau Varilla Treaty.
This judgment was modified and affirmed (in 160 F. 2d 131), which does not add anything of particular interest to Judge Gardner's tour de force. (3)

177
Robert J. Fleming, Jr., Governor of the Canal Zone Government and Cyrus R. Vance, Secretary of the Army in his supervisory capacity for the administration of the Canal Zone Government, Defendants, Civ. no. 5456. District Court, Canal Zone, Division Balboa, July 8, 1963. Federal supplement; cases argued and determined in the District Courts of the United States and the United States Customs Court v. 219, 1963: 277–285.   LL

This was primarily an action pleading for an injunction to restrain the governor from displaying the Panamanian flag on or about any public building in the Canal Zone, as had been agreed to by the president. The complaint was dismissed on the constitutional grounds that a citizen has no right to challenge the conduct of foreign affairs in the court.
Nevertheless, the language of the decision tends to question the wisdom of the policy decision of the executive and to raise consciousness that sensitive issues of sovereignty are involved: "The people living in the Canal Zone are entitled to police protection, adequate courts, orderly government, health programs and all of the things that stem from the sovereign. When the sovereign is uncertain and in doubt these fundamental rights are of necessity weakened and may be lost." Resistance to the flag policy by the zonians, which cannot fail to have been encouraged by this decision, was the immediate cause of the riots of January 1964. (2)

K. Decisions of the Supreme Court of Panama

178
Petición ... seguido por Juan Gris contra la Compañía Nueva del Canal de Panamá [J. N. Gris v. The New Panama Canal Company] 2 *Registro Judicial* 59 (1905).   LL

In Spanish.

In this decision, rendered on January 20, 1905, the *Corte Suprema de Justicia de Panamá,* citing articles 3 and 16 of the Hay-Bunau Varilla Treaty, conceded the "rights of the United States to organize, to the exclusion of the Republic of Panama, the Judiciary of the Canal Zone ...." (1)

179
Juicio ejecutivo seguido por Carlos Carbone contra Juan Esquivel [Carlos Carbone v. Juan Esquivel] 2 *Registro Judicial* 61 (1905).   LL

In Spanish.

In this decision, rendered on January 25, 1905, the *Corte Suprema de Justicia de Panamá* followed and reinforced the precedent of Gris (entry 178) as to the treaty rights of the United States to administer justice in the zone. It also took note, however, of the contention of the *procurador general* [attorney general] of Panama that the republic retained its rights of sovereignty in the zone and "therefore the Judges of Panama have not lost their jurisdiction in cases triable by them prior to the American ... possession of the Canal Zone, though such cases may cover real-estate situated therein." (1)

180
Auto contra Kenneth Robert Bartlett, por rapto [charge against Kenneth Robert Bartlett, for rape] 28.1 *Registro Judicial* 136 (1930).   LL

In Spanish.

The defendant was accused of having committed rape in the Republic of Panama, but at the time action was commenced against him he was living in the Canal Zone. The Panamanian court of first instance attempted to have him returned for trial by following the procedure prescribed in article 815 of the Judicial Code; viz., by addressing a request for extradition to the Ministry of Foreign Affairs. In this decision the Supreme Court of Panama said that that was the wrong procedure because "the Canal Zone is not foreign territory." The proper procedure, the court said, was to invoke article 16 of the Hay-Bunau Varilla Treaty which provided a modus operandi for such cases. (1)

L. Colombia: Ministry of Foreign Affairs

181
The Panama Canal question, a plea for Colombia. New York, 1904. 129 p.   TC774.A36
Much of the material in this collection corresponds to Abelardo Aldano's pamphlet: *The Panama Canal Question: a Plea for Colombia.* 2d ed., enl. (Cardiff, 1903. TC774.A35).
Contents: The Panama Canal question, by Abelardo Aldano.—Appendix to the former article.—Diplomatic notes between the Minister of the United States at Bogotá and the Colombia Minister of Foreign Affairs, from November 11th to November 21st, 1903.—Colombia and the Hay-Herran Treaty, by Antonio Llano.—Was Panama ever an independent state?—The logic of the message.—Did the Treaty of 1846 give any advantages to the United States?—Duty, not right.—The path of justice.—Violation of a treaty, by Francisco Escobar.—Colombia guiltless of extortion.—Presidents on the New Granada Treaty.—English opinions.—New diplomatic notes between the Secretary of State and the Minister of Colombia on Special Mission, from December 23d, 1903, to January 13th, 1904.
The statement of the contents, above, makes any annotation almost superfluous. Suffice it to say that this book makes an effective presentation of the case for Colombia against the United States in the Panamanian affair. Though no author or publisher is shown, it was undoubtedly published under the auspices of the Colombian Ministry of Foreign Relations. (1)

182
Colombia. *Ministerio de Relaciones Exteriores.* Protest of Colombia against the treaty between Panama and the United States. London, Printed by Wertheimer, Lea, 1904. 44 p.
F1566.5C77 1904a
This is another polemic which is also very effective, similar in thrust and purpose to entry

181. It concentrates on the argument that the United States, by entering into the Hay-Bunau Varilla Treaty, violated the Treaty of 1846 and the "rules of neutrality established by the Law of Nations." Unlike entry 181, however, which is simply an anonymous broadcast to the world, this issuance is an official communiqué to the chargé d'affaires ad interim of the United States in Bogotá from the Colombian Minister of Foreign Relations. (1)

M. Congressional Research Service Issuances

183
U.S. *Library of Congress. Foreign Affairs Division.* Disposal by treaty of United States property rights in Panama [by] Rieck B. Hannifin. [Washington] 1967. 39 p.   CRS
"JX1428 For. Latin America."
A highly uncertain and sensitive element in the internal controversy over a new Panama Canal treaty is the question of whether property rights in the existing Canal Zone can be transferred to the Republic of Panama by a self-executing treaty alone or whether enacting legislation by the whole Congress would be required. Opponents of any change in the status quo are the most vocal exponents of the latter view, relying on article IV, number 3, clause 2 of the Constitution which provides: "The Congress shall have power to dispose of and make all needful rules and regulations respecting the territory or other property belonging to the United States. . . ." The official Department of State position seems to be that no implementing legislation would be necessary, and historically there are several precedents for the disposition of property by treaty. There are arguments and precedents on both sides, however, and the issue has never been explicitly decided.
The question is referred to in several other entries in this bibliography, but this is the only one devoted exclusively to the subject. It is a scholarly, thorough, and impartial study. (1)

184
——Panama-United States relations since the riots of 1959 [by] Rieck B. Hannifin. Washington, 1967. 43 p.   CRS
"F–250."
Touches upon all the important high spots in Panama-United States relations, specifically including the riots of January 1964, from the riots of 1959 to August 1967. All the factual information in it can be found, of course, in other places, but this document neatly ties together in easily readable form all consequential events within the stated subject and the time frame. (2)

185

——Negotiation of new Panama Canal treaties: background and pros and cons [by] Virginia M. Hagen. [Washington] 1971. 30 p.   CRS "71–250F."

A sound and clear, though very brief, synopsis of the main grounds of contention between the two parties, with historical emphasis on events from 1964 to 1971. Supplements entries 183 and 184. (2).

186

U.S. *Library of Congress. Foreign Affairs and National Defense Division*. Panama Canal. Author: Storrs, K. Larry [and] Sklar, Barry A. [Washington] 1977. 30 p. (Issue brief no. IB74138)   CRS

Issue briefs are designed to present concise summaries of information on key policy and legislative aspects of specific problems. They are periodically updated by Congressional Research Service analysts. This is the latest update of the brief on the Panama Canal. All future updatings will carry the same issue brief number. (1)

N. International Organizations

187

U.S. *Dept. of State*. The United States and non-self-governing territories. A summary of information regarding the United States and non-self-governing territories with particular reference to chapters XI, XII, and XIII of the Charter of the United Nations. Washington, U.S. Govt. Print. Off., 1947. 106 p. fold. col. map. (*Its* Publication 2812. United States-United Nations information series, 18)

JX4021.U5 1947a

See page 21 of this publication. In accordance with provisions of the UN Charter concerning non-self-governing territories, the Department of State transmitted to the Secretary General of the United Nations on August 19, 1946, "copies of the latest Annual Reports of the Governors of Alaska, Hawaii, Puerto Rico, the Virgin Islands, and the Panama Canal Zone." The Delegation of Panama asserted that the United States should not have included the Canal Zone among the territories for which it submitted information under article 73(e) of the charter, "chiefly on the grounds that sovereignty over the Canal Zone resides in the Republic of Panama." (1)

188

United Nations. *General Assembly*. Delegation of Panama: Declaration regarding inclusion of the Panama Canal Zone in the report made by the United States in the matter of non-self-governing territories (Article 73(e) of the Charter)

[New York?] 1946. 7 p. (United Nations [Document] A/200. 26 Nov. 1946)

JX1977.A2 A/200

This is the full declaration of the Delegation of Panama protesting the report of the United States referred to in entry 187. It includes the statement: "The strip of land known as the Panama Canal Zone has neither been purchased, nor conquered, nor annexed, nor ceded, nor leased, nor its sovereignty transferred by Panama to the United States." It also points out, as one of the reasons for the inapplicability of article 73(e), that the Canal Zone has "no permanent population . . . that aspires to self-government or independence or can attain one or the other." (1)

189

Inter-American Peace Committee. Situation between Panama and the United States of America (January 1964). *In its* Report to the Second Special Inter-American Conference on the activities of the Committee since the Tenth Inter-American Conference, 1954–1965. Washington, Pan American Union, 1965. (OEA/ser.L/III/II.10(English)) p. 49–53.

Micro OAS Doc. microfiche OEA/ser.L/III/II.10

When serious rioting broke out along the Panama Canal Zone border on January 9, 1964, the representatives of Panama and the United States on the Council of the Organization of American States requested the Inter-American Peace Committee to take action. The Committee succeeded in restoring tranquility and issued a statement on January 15, 1964, to the effect that the parties had agreed, within thirty days after diplomatic relations are reestablished, "to discuss without limitations all existing matters of any nature which may affect the relations between the United States and Panama." This was the opening wedge in the process which led eventually to the reestablishment of diplomatic relations (entry 139) and the commitment of President Johnson to a new treaty (entry 140). (2)

190

International Commission of Jurists (*Founded 1952*). Report on the events in Panama, January 9–12, 1964. Prepared by the investigating committee appointed by the International Commission of Jurists. Geneva [1964] 46 p. maps.

E183.8.P2155

Released June 10, 1964.

Following the riots of January 1964, the International Commission of Jurists (ICJ) was requested by the National Bar Association of Panama to investigate complaints that the military actions of the United States during the disturbance had violated articles 3, 5, and 20 of the Universal Declaration of Human Rights. The ICJ appointed an investigating committee which, after a thorough examination, rejected the complaints as unsubstantiated and found that the United States had used no more force than was necessary for self-defense.

The investigating committee also, however, looked into the underlying causes of the buildup of tension which preceded the riots, pointing out that:

The issue of the interpretation of the Convention of 1903 is, therefore, not an abstract problem but of great practical importance. Modifications in the 1903 treaty were made in 1936, 1942, 1947 and 1955. The main problem, however, remains unresolved; indeed it is this problem which gave rise to the subject matter of the current difficulties.

The practical importance of the pinpointed issue is no less today than it was in 1964, but it has been subsumed in the larger issue of whether, and if so, how, to replace the 1903 convention entirely with a new treaty. (1)

III. Legal Treatises

The entries in this genus (with few exceptions) were written by, and primarily for, lawyers—in most cases international lawyers, or law professors. Consequently, they tend to be more specialized than the other types of material in this bibliography and may present some difficulties for nonlawyers; yet they are not, by and large, so abstruse that the average intelligent layman cannot follow the reasoning and decide for himself to what extent he agrees with the author. In any case, these entries cannot fail to add something to the reader's store of knowledge on the subject.

In order to keep this bibliography within reasonable bounds, the treatises are limited to some of those published in American law journals in English, but includes enough to be representative of every important legal issue. Also, it is felt that fairness is not lost by such seeming parochialism; several of the treatises herewith, though written by American authors, present the Panamanian (and Colombian) case fully and forcefully.

The entries are presented in chronological order so that the reader can watch the legal argumentation develop in historical context.

191
Grant, Charles R. The Panama Canal and the Monroe Doctrine. The Southern law review, n.s., v. 6, Dec. 1880: 729–761.　　　K23.079, n.s., v. 6

In a special message to Congress on March 8, 1880, President Hayes declared: "The policy of this country is a canal under American control . . . ." Concurrently, various committees of the Congress were issuing ringing, and sometimes gratuitously provocative, statements to the same effect; both the executive and legislative branches basing their positions on the supposition that the building of a canal by any European power would be a violation of the Monroe Doctrine.

The author of this article argues that the assertion of such a position cannot be supported by any reasonable interpretation of the Monroe Doctrine; and even if it could, it would be fatuous for the nation to be making threats which it is not militarily capable of enforcing. This is quite possibly the earliest legal treatise to deal seriously with the applicability of the Monroe Doctrine to the American claim of exclusive canal rights.

It should also be remembered that the Clayton-Bulwer Treaty was still in effect at the time, and no active movement to abrogate it was under way.

A French-owned company began digging a canal across the Isthmus of Panama in 1881, and continued digging for several years without interference by the United States (but see entry 92). (2)

192
Hyde, Charles Cheney. Recent Isthmian Canal negotiations. Yale law journal, v. 10, June 1901: 315–321.　　　K29.A4, v. 10

The "recent" canal negotiations which Professor Hyde writes about in this article were those between the United States and Great Britain which resulted in the first Hay-Pauncefote Treaty wherein the United States sought to obtain a free hand to build and maintain a canal without the restraints of the Clayton-Bulwer Treaty. The first Hay-Pauncefote Treaty had been rejected and the successful second not yet negotiated, so it may be said, in a sense, that this article had a very short life span and is not worth mentioning; but that would not be quite true because of its perceptive appreciation of the progress made in establishing the rule of law:

This country has ... declared to England ... that it still recognizes the binding character of the Clayton-Bulwer Treaty. This has been a direct result of the isthmian canal negotiations .... It removes all objection to the giving of a consideration for the acquisition of greater rights in the isthmus. The solution of the problem has been hastened .... (2)

193
Hawes, Herbert B. The recognition of Panama. Law notes, v. 7, Dec. 1903: 167–169.   LL

The distinction of this entry is that it was apparently the first analysis of the subject to appear in a prestigious law journal after the secession of Panama, and it precipitated recognition by the United States. Written even before the perfection of the Hay-Bunau Varilla Treaty, it is obviously not a product of long reflection, but rather a spontaneous reaction—almost a part of the res gestae if the meaning of the term may be stretched a little.

There is something timeless—almost as insightful in 1976 as the day it was written—in the way the author agonizes over the recognition: on the one hand finding it indefensible in precedent and international law, and on the other taking satisfaction in the result (p. 169): "It is safe even to say that the majority of the people of the United States are glad at heart that Panama has revolted and has been recognized, provided this will hasten the construction of a canal . . . ."

He closes with the following wistful appeasement of conscience (p. 169):

Congress has asked for the papers in the matter, and it is sincerely hoped that these papers will furnish a complete justification of our, at present writing, seemingly high-handed conduct towards a weaker sister republic, and thus give legal and moral support to our nation in the accomplishment of her manifest destiny. (1)

194
Woolsey, Theodore S. The recognition of Panama and its results. The Green bag, v. 16, Jan. 1904: 6–12.   LL

This is apparently the second jurisprudential reaction to recognition (see entry 193). Also written before the perfection of the Hay-Bunau Varilla Treaty (and before the adoption by Panama of a constitutional form of government), it is a product of somewhat more reflection and is a little more profound, but expresses substantially the same view as Hawes that "our recognition of Panama was warranted neither by law nor by treaty."

The author (who was then professor of international law at Yale), then propounds the inquiry (p. 11): "Is our canal treaty, made with Panama under the Junta, valid, and title to property leased or ceded by it, good?"

He answers the question with the final of several conclusions (p. 12): "The canal treaty, negotiated and ratified by the Junta, with no constitutional authority or other authorization, is of doubtful validity and the defect will need to be subsequently cured." (1)

195
Crangle, Roland. Legal aspects of the Panama question. The American lawyer, v. 12, May 1904: 214–217; June: 251–253.   LL

This article rambles a bit, for a legal treatise, but offers enough juridical foundation to support the author's key proposition that (p. 252): "As to the recognition of the independence of Panama, it is in direct conflict with the neutral policy heretofore observed by the United States, and it is not sustained by any of the authorities on international law."

However, he also says, speaking of Pres. Theodore Roosevelt (p. 252–253): "I believe that the policy he has adopted in this Panama dispute has been with a sincere conviction that he was doing right and, as he says, advancing 'the interests of the civilized world.' "

Remembering that this article was written, not only after perfection of the Hay-Bunau Varilla Treaty but even after the physical transfer of French property on the isthmus had made the matter a fait accompli, the last paragraph has a quixotic sound as if the author still does not realize that the moving finger has writ and having writ, moved on (p. 253):

The commission of an international wrong by a Republic that for more than a century has been the hope and the inspiration of mankind in the experiment of self-government, will be much more of an injury to civilization, in its true sense, than will the postponement for a few years more or less, of the construction of a canal between the Atlantic and Pacific. (2)

196
Dennis, William C. The Panama situation in the light of international law. The American law register, v. 52, May 1904: 265–306.

K25.N69, v. 52

A detailed, meticulous, and finely reasoned study of article 35 of the Treaty of 1846, and the application thereof, as the author says (p. 266), "from a purely legal standpoint . . . to the occurrences between the date of the revolution and the recognition by the United States of the independence of Panama. With the political and ethical questions involved we have nothing to do." With respect to the crucial action of the U.S. government in preventing the Colombian soldiers at Colón from moving to Panama City to suppress the insurrection, the author concludes (p. 306): "This was an act of political intervention; its justification must be found in considerations of ethics and expediency. It cannot be found in law." Nevertheless, the author makes it clear that, in his opinion, the extra legal considerations were overriding and therefore the course taken by the government was amply justified. (2)

197
Williams, Charles R. The legal status of the Panama Canal Zone. The American lawyer, v. 15, Mar. 1907: 125–127.   LL

Almost entirely expository, this short article adds very little to the legal literature on the canal. After a highly condensed and eclectic, but accurate, history, the author sets up and answers these questions: (a) "Has the United States a good title to the Panama Canal Zone?" Williams answers yes. (b) "What is the status of the Panama Canal Zone and its inhabitants with reference to the United States? What are the powers of Congress in legislating for the Canal Zone? To what extent do the Constitution and Laws of the United States apply to the Canal Zone? In short, does the Constitution follow the flag?" This question, in its short form, is not specifically answered but it may be inferred, from the description of the form of government, that the answer is no.

A great deal of correct information packed into a very little space is the only reason for this entry's being. (3)

198
Hains, Peter C. Neutralization of the Panama Canal. The American journal of international law, v. 3, Apr. 1909: 354–394.   LL

This article, though concerning an issue long ago overtaken by events, is still of some interest. The questions of neutralization and fortification, as elements in the context of defense of the canal, remain factors in the overall fabric of canal treaty relationships. The author was a former member of the Isthmian Canal Commission and also of the first and second Walker commissions. The kernel of his thesis can be summed up in two quotations:

It is believed that it can be shown that the Hay-Pauncefote Treaty imposes on the United States, inferentially at least, the obligation to abstain from the erection of fortifications; but that whether it does, or does not, the advantages derived from them are so insignificant that it is better policy not to construct them. (p. 354)

Nothing short of the most imperious necessity would therefore justify the United States in constructing them, and no such necessity exists. (p. 394) (2)

199
Davis, George W. Fortification at Panama. The American journal of international law, v. 3, Oct. 1909: 885–908.   LL

An answer to entry 198, this article takes a diametrically opposed view. The author was the first governor of the Canal Zone (and being a major general outranked Hains who was only a brigadier general). His conclusions are (p. 908):

1. It is the declared policy of the United States to control and defend the canal as a part of the coastline of the United States.

2. Neither public law nor moral obligations are in conflict with this policy.

3. Fortifications at Panama are as essential to the protection of our national interests as they are on our coasts which by the canal are brought 8,400 miles nearer the one to the other. (2)

200
Knapp, H. S. The real status of the Panama Canal as regards neutralization. The American journal of international law, v. 4, Apr. 1910: 314–358.   LL

Another answer to entry 198, taking no notice, for some unknown reason, of the fact that it had already been answered by General Davis (entry 199) in October 1909. It is not completely supererogatory, however, as it ranges rather more widely into the international law of interoceanic waterways and adds a little more weight to the arguments adduced by Davis, while coming to the same conclusion (p. 358): "It is the duty of the United States to erect and garrison permanent defenses for the protection of the canal." (2)

201
Olney, Richard. Fortification of the Panama Canal. The American journal of international law, v. 5, Apr. 1911: 298–301.   LL

A brief treatise which does not contribute much but follows the debate over neutralization of the canal into 1911. The author purports to find in the Clayton-Bulwer and Hay-Pauncefote treaties persuasive inference of intent to keep the canal neutral and unfortified. Thus he aligns himself with Hains (entry 198). (3)

202
Wambaugh, Eugene. The right to fortify the Panama Canal. The American journal of international law, v. 5, July 1911: 615–619.   LL

This brief article concludes that the United States does have the right to fortify. Although the author does not find this view inconsistent with the Hay-Pauncefote Treaty, he believes the right does not spring from that agreement but rather from the Hay-Bunau Varilla Treaty, since Panama, rather than Great Britain, is the only source capable of conferring such a right. (2)

203
Kennedy, Crammond. The Canal fortifications and the treaty. The American journal of international law, v. 5, July 1911: 620–638.   LL

This entry amounts to a brief against fortification, but is founded more on considerations of sound policy than of legality or illegality; though the author does say that "the right 'to establish fortifications,' as defined by the United States itself, in its treaty with Panama, is not a right *in presenti* but *in futuro*" and depends on the arising of some necessity. He prefers to assume—with what in hindsight sounds like an unworldly idealism—that such a necessity will never arise.

The author takes issue with an article by Admiral Mahan favoring fortification which appeared a few months earlier (entry 249). (2)

204

Latane, John Holladay. The Panama Canal Act and the British protest. The American journal of international law, v. 7, Jan. 1913: 17–26.

LL

The Panama Canal Act of 1912 exempted American ships in the coastwise trade from the payment of tolls, in contravention of the Hay-Pauncefote Treaty of 1901 which provided that the canal should be open to the vessels of "all nations . . . on terms of entire equality." Great Britain protested, and that complaint is what this article is about. As Panama itself was not involved, except as one of "all nations," this entry is of only marginal relevance to the subject of this bibliography.

The offending provision of the Panama Canal Act was repealed by Congress in 1914 at the request of President Wilson. (3)

[Compiler's note: The canal was opened for commerce on August 15, 1914—about three weeks before the outbreak of World War I, which suddenly wrenched the whole subject of neutralization and fortification out of its academic womb into the cold pragmatic world of action. All the entries in this genus up to this point, including entry 204, were precanal, so to speak, as well as prewar.]

205

A Caribbean policy for the United States. The American journal of international law, v. 8, Oct. 1914: 886–889.   JX1.A6, v. 8

LL

This entry appears in the "Editorial Comment" section of the journal. It points out that it was no coincidence that the Platt Amendment (reserving the right of the United States to intervene in Cuba "for the preservation of Cuban independence, the maintenance of a government adequate for the protection of life, property, and individual liberty") was conceived and drafted in 1901 by Secretary of War Elihu Root at the same time that other diplomatic maneuvers were clearing the way for an American-controlled canal in Panama. The thrust of this comment is that the canal was the corner-

stone of U.S. Caribbean policy of the period; the approaches to the canal must be safeguarded.

The connection between the Platt Amendment and the canal is cogently expressed in the following excerpt from the editorial comment (p. 889):

The United States desires the independence of Cuba; it also desires the independence of the republics in the Caribbean and to the north of the canal. It wishes a government in Cuba adequate to maintain its independence and to guarantee life, liberty and the protection of property. It also wishes such a government in the republics in the Caribbean and to the north of the canal, not merely because it is interested in the independence of these republics, and in constitutional government generally, but also because the islands are within a stone's throw, as it were, of our territory, and because the countries to the north of the canal must be independent and orderly governments, if the canal is to be useful not merely to the United States and to them, but to the world at large.

There are unspoken overtones in the appearance of this comment, with its emphasis on safeguarding approaches to the canal, so soon after the beginning of World War I had shattered a long period of world peace (in which the fleeting Spanish-American War made hardly a ripple) and shaken up the long-range, optimistic expectations of policy planners. (1)

206

Woolsey, L. H. The sovereignty of the Panama Canal Zone. The American journal of international law, v. 20, Jan. 1926: 117–124.

JX1.A6, v. 20
LL

Another "Editorial Comment," this treatise is a learned and evenhanded study of the perennial and undying subject denominated in the title, with particular attention to the conflict between articles II and III of the Hay-Bunau Varilla Treaty and the question of whether the former has a limiting effect on the latter. The editorial comment concludes:

It is not derogatory of the views entertained by either party to say that it was doubtless not the intention of either party that the United States should hold and administer the Canal Zone as an independent colony or possession of the United States. The Canal Zone is more in the nature of a great international right of way across Panama territory, of which the United States is the administrator and protector with power sufficient to carry out the great design of the parties.

The author was a former president of the American Society of International Law, and an honorary vice president at the time of his death in 1929.

This article was translated into Spanish and reproduced in the leading Panama City newspaper, *La Estrella de Panamá*. It was heavily relied on in at least two of the articles by Panamanian jurists in entry 54. (1)

207
Padelford, Norman J. American rights in the Panama Canal. The American journal of international law, v. 34, July 1940: 416–442.   LL

This article, written during World War II but while the United States was still officially neutral, reexamines, more thoroughly and with benefit of another thirty years of hindsight, the questions of fortification and neutralization so vigorously but inconclusively debated in the precanal period (entries 198–203). The author also provides a clear and useful analysis of the basic legal situation respecting both the Canal Zone and the canal, recognizing, as much of the current public disputation over a new treaty does not, the distinctness of the subjects. He purposefully limits the scope to an "examination of the treaties and laws fundamental to American rights in the Isthmus of Panama, and which came into force prior to the commencement of the construction of the Panama Canal by the United States."

The author was a professor of international law at the Fletcher School of Law and Diplomacy (see also entry 52). (1)

208
——The Panama Canal in time of peace. The American journal of international law, v. 34, Oct. 1940: 601–637.   LL

This is the second article in a trilogy, the first of which was entry 207. It is of equal quality and significance. With the admonition to keep in mind the legal framework as explained in the first article, the reader is told that the second and third articles will "examine in detail the laws, executive orders, regulations, decisions, and agreements which have attended the operation and control of the Canal in peace and war." This article delivers on that promise. While a substantial portion of it deals with navigational and other matters of limited relevance to current treaty negotiations, it also contains some highly pertinent material, and in any case is an essential link in the trilogy. One of the many interesting questions examined is whether the neutralization of the Canal, provided for in the Hay-Pauncefote Treaty, applies to the airspace above the Canal Zone. (1)

209
——Neutrality, belligerency, and the Panama Canal. The American journal of international law, v. 35, Jan. 1941: 55–89.   LL

The final article in a trilogy (see entries 207 and 208). It is simply a continuation of the first two with a shift in emphasis to wartime prob-

lems. A careful reading of the trilogy, and especially of this last part, should be a required precedent to any serious discussion of the military and defense aspects of a new canal treaty. (1)

210
Woolsey, L. H. Executive agreements relating to Panama. American journal of international law, v. 37, July 1943: 482–489.   LL

Appearing as an "Editorial Comment," this treatise is rather in the nature of an exegesis of the executive agreements of May 18, 1942 (entry 156). It is mostly expository but touches on such legal points as the possible reversionary rights of Colombia and the distinction between treaties and executive agreements. (3)

211
García-Mora, Manuel R. International law applicable to the defense of the Panama Canal. University of Detroit law journal, v. 12, Jan. 1949:   63–73.
      K25.N58, v. 12
      LL

This article is illustrative of some of the pitfalls and difficulties involved in drafting agreements relating to the defense of the canal. The specific incident discussed adverts to the granting of the use of certain defense sites provided for in the executive agreement of 1942 (see entry 156, last paragraph of annotation), and the application thereto of article X of the general treaty of friendship and cooperation of 1936 (see entry 155). (2)

212
N. K. Applicability of Federal statutes to noncontiguous areas. University of Pennsylvania law review, v. 97, May 1949: 866–877.   K25.N69
      LL

A close examination of the problems arising from interpretation of statutory coverage of noncontiguous areas over which the United States exercises varying degrees of control. The areas treated are classified as:

(1) owned areas under exclusive United States sovereignty;
(2) *the Panama Canal Zone—an anomaly* [italics added];
(3) areas leased by the owner-State to the United States;
(4) trusteeship territories; and
(5) areas occupied by military forces.

Without making a special point of it, but simply letting the facts speak for themselves, this article strikingly illustrates the "anomalous" status of the Canal Zone.

After pointing out some of the confusion and inconsistency in the determination of the zone's status by our own government, the article concludes: "The strategic and commercial implications inherent in any conflicts and inconsistencies that arise, appear to be the prime factors affecting their disposition, the agreement with the Republic of Panama being comprehensive enough to give this country a free hand in their solution." (2)

213
Ealy, Lawrence. The development of an Anglo-American system of law in the Panama Canal Zone. American journal of legal history, v. 2, Oct. 1958: 283–303.   LL

A brief, compact review of the conflict of laws in the Canal Zone and the eventual triumph of the Anglo-American common law system over the preexisting Spanish-American legal system grounded in the Roman civil law. As the author points out, although the Hay-Bunau Varilla Treaty did not say anything specifically about the legal system which should be applicable in the zone, it contained language broad enough to permit the United States to exercise all the rights, power, and authority it would possess "if it were the sovereign" of the territory. Peculiarities and anomalies arose from the fact that the United States chose to exercise this authority gradually, retaining "the law of the land with which the inhabitants are familiar," but progressively modifying that law to conform to common law principles and practice. The result was that for a good many years the two legal systems coexisted and there was a good deal of unpredictability as to how specific cases would be decided.

By 1958, when this article was written, the transformation was almost, but not quite, complete. The author concludes:

> When one considers that here is a completely totalitarian state in the economic and political sense, yet operated by the world's greatest democracy; that despite this totalitarianism the great rights which English-speaking man has won for himself since the time of Magna Carta are preserved, honored, and enjoyed; that this whole Anglo-American structure of courts and law is superimposed upon the base of a Latin American-Roman tradition which endures in significant form; then one can surely conclude that the Panama Canal Zone is the most unusual jurisdiction under the flag of the United States! (2)

214
Weiner, Richard M. Sovereignty of the Panama Isthmus. Intramural law review of New York University, School of Law, v. 16, Nov. 1960: 65–76.   LL

This article was prompted by Panamanian Law 58 of December 1958 which purported to extend the territorial sea of Panama (including that of the Canal Zone) from three to twelve miles. The author quickly cuts through the intermediate issues raised thereby and gets to the fundamental problem: Who is the sovereign

of the isthmus? He does not answer the question, implying that it may be unanswerable in conventional terms—"any conventional label may be misleading for our position is *sui generis*" (p. 67)—but contributes some highly useful thoughts.

In exploring, and rejecting, the proposition that the Hay-Bunau Varilla Treaty may be a "disguised cession," the author makes a comparison with the Chinese leases of 1898; one of the few writers on the subject to do so (see also entry 9). (1)

215
Hanrahan, David G. Legal aspects of the Panama Canal Zone: in perspective. Boston University law review, v. 45, winter 1965: 64–87.   LL

A law review "note" that goes over much familiar ground but is well worth reading nevertheless, partly because it is one of the first (see also entry 216) comprehensive legal reexaminations after the commitment of President Johnson in December 1964 to abrogate the 1903 treaty and negotiate a new one. It is a combination of condensed history and legal analysis. The author is no more successful than any other publicist in solving the problem of sovereignty, but seems to look with favor on modern theorists who regard the traditional view of sovereignty as (p. 80) "an overworked fiction which no longer is essential to the concept of the state." (1)

216
Hunt, E. L. Roy. The Panama Canal treaties: past, present, future. University of Florida law review, v. 18, winter 1965: 398–429

K25.N6, v. 18
LL

Like entry 215, this law review article appeared shortly after, and makes specific reference to, the commitment of President Johnson in December 1964 to abrogate the 1903 treaty and negotiate a new one. Its uniqueness lies in the fact that it uses the terminology and the distinctive analytical approach initiated by and associated with Prof. Myres McDougal of Yale University. Thus, the whole subject is considered in the light of the McDougal concepts of world public order, which makes it unusually interesting and different.

Consistent with the McDougal line of thought, the author poses these three broad but interrelated questions:

(1) Why has the world community made no move toward internationalizing the Panama Canal, thus assuring the most inclusive possible use of such a vital waterway?
(2) Why has Panama taken no unilateral action to terminate the Hay-Bunau Varilla Treaty of 1903?
(3) Why is the United States negotiating a new treaty if it under no legal compulsion to so do?

The reader will find the answers absorbing and stimulating, whether or not he agrees. (1)

217

Hoyt, Edwin C. Law and politics in the revision of treaties affecting the Panama Canal. Virginia journal of international law, v. 6, Apr. 1966: 289–309.   LL

The takeoff point for this article was the simultaneous release by President Johnson and President Robles of Panama on September 24, 1965, of an announcement of the attainment of areas of agreement for a new treaty (entry 141) which would unequivocally abrogate the Hay-Bunau Varilla Treaty. The author obviously considers that a desirable and inevitable development. While giving due weight to the *law*, the emphasis in this article is on the *politics* involved in the revision of treaties (p. 290):

The old treaty no longer accords with the balance of political power and interests of the two parties. It has become so unacceptable to Panamanian nationalists that they are no longer willing peacefully to accept it, and they now find many influential political allies outside Panama. The treaty regime, after a time lag, is being brought into accord with these political realities. If it were not capable of the adjustment the treaty would lose its political relevance. The danger is that the illusion of being protected by clearcut legal rights may have delayed too long the political accommodation which practical interests demand. (1)

218

Padelford, Norman J. Ocean commerce and the Panama Canal. Journal of maritime law and commerce, v. 4, no. 3, Apr. 1973: 397–423.
K10.088
LL

Professor Padelford has been a recognized authority on the Panama Canal for more than thirty years and has contributed significantly to the discussion of the treaty problem. This particular article is of only marginal relevance as it is mostly concerned with commercial and navigational matters. He does, however, touch briefly on the treaty controversy (p. 401):

Notwithstanding the concessions that have been made on activities within the Zone, the latter still remains firmly within the grip of the United States Government. No concessions have been made on the fundamentals of U.S. operation and control of the Canal and Canal Zone Government. These are not likely to come about until Washington takes a decision at the highest Congressional and Executive levels to admit Panama to participation in the control. This will meet strenuous objection both in the Congress and within the Department of Defense.

Another point of interest is the author's conclusion that it would be in the long-run interests of the United States to construct the proposed sea-level canal. (3)

219

Mazer, Alan D. Panama Canal treaty—statement of principles provides guidelines for negotiation of new Panama Canal treaty in complete abrogation of 1903 treaty as amended—joint statement of the Honorable Henry A. Kissinger, Secretary of State of the United States of America, and His Excellency Juan Antonio Tack, Minister of Foreign Affairs of the Republic of Panama, on February 7, 1974. Vanderbilt journal of transnational law, v. 7, no. 3, summer 1974: 744–749.
LL

In commenting on the Kissinger-Tack joint statement of February 7, 1974 (entry 145), this short article points out that it was not the first document of its kind; (p. 748) "more than eight years ago, on September 24, 1965, President Johnson of the United States and President Robles of Panama signed an agreement that contained most of the same general provisions." The author therefore concludes (p. 749):

If, indeed, a change in United States policy toward Latin America has occurred, the new policy will be vigorously tested in the months and years to come. In the light of our past history and the difficult problems that remain unsolved, it would seem that a great deal of time, effort, and "partnership" will be required before any new relationship between the United States and Panama is finally created. (3)

220

Simpson, Michael D. Panama: the proposed transfer of the Canal and Canal Zone by treaty. Georgia journal of international and comparative law, v. 5, no. 1, 1975: 195–215. K7.E65, v. 5
LL

This article addresses, and thoroughly examines, the question of whether the canal and the Canal Zone, together with property therein, can be transferred to Panama by treaty, or whether some concurrent and enabling legislation by the whole Congress is required. As the author correctly observes (p. 196): "The conflict is a constitutional controversy of the highest order." Those who argue that the House must participate rely on article IV, number 3, clause 2 of the Constitution: "Congress shall have power to dispose of . . . the territory or other property belonging to the United States." For the position taken by the Panama Canal Subcommittee of the House Committee on Merchant Marine and Fisheries, see entry 127, p. 21.

The author gives the arguments and precedents on both sides of the question and comes to the following conclusion as a matter of constitutional law (p. 214):

Even if one accepts the proposition that only the Congress can transfer United States property under the constitution, the inevitable conclusion is that there is no way the House can prevent the President and the Senate from transferring the Canal and the Canal Zone to

Panama once the decision is made to make such a transfer. The House has a right but no means of enforcing that right. (1)

221
Norberg, Charles R. U.S. Panama negotiations for a new canal treaty. Federal bar news, v. 23, Apr. 1976: 101–105.   LL

Albeit short, this article is a fair and exceptionally lucid summation of the situation respecting the new canal treaty controversy as of April 1976. The urgency of the problem, and the sense of injustice strongly felt by Panamanians, are clearly conveyed; but the difficulty which the executive will have in persuading Congress to go along with commitments already made is not minimized. The author is president of the Inter-American Bar Foundation, which, together with the Fletcher School of Law and Diplomacy and other concerned organizations, presented a seminar on the subject in Washington, D.C., on May 27, 1976. As the author correctly points out, there is much misunderstanding of even the basic facts involved in the controversy, so the purpose of the seminar was educational. (2)

IV. Manuscript Collections

The following manuscript collections, in the Library of Congress Manuscript Division, contain primary source material relevant to the subject of this bibliography. It would be impossible, within any feasible time limitation, to locate and identify every such item. The Manuscript Division will be happy to assist any serious researcher, however, and the collections are efficiently arranged for easy accessibility.

222
Bunau-Varilla papers. Bunau-Varilla, Philippe, 1859–1940. Papers 1880/1955. 40 containers, 10,000 items

222a
Bunau-Varilla, Philippe. The revelations of the Congressional document entitled "The Story of Panama-Hearings on the Rainey Resolution before the Committee on Foreign Affairs of the House of Representatives-Washington Govt. Printing Office 1913". [1938] 24 1. Mss
Typescript.
Bunau-Varilla papers, box 16.
"A study made by Mr. Philippe Bunau-Varilla for the Library of Congress to accompany his personal documents on the creation of the Republic of Panama and on the Hay Bunau-Varilla treaty, now being forwarded to the Library-Paris July 26, 1938."—Leaf 1.

Included in the same folder is a slightly longer (32-page) version of the above, broken down into six chapters and a conclusion, with a table of contents.

In this document, written shortly before his death and twenty-six years after the main event, Bunau-Varilla gets in the last word in his long feud with Cromwell. A kind of postscript to entry 111. (2)

223
Dillen papers. Dillen, Roscoe Franklin, 1881–1946. Naval officer. Papers, 1925–27. 45 items.

Memorandum prepared by Dillen for the director of the U.S. Army War College on "Negotiations Leading Up to the Building of the Panama Canal." Deposited by the Naval Historical Foundation, 1969. (2)

224
Hay papers. Hay, John, 1838–1905. Papers, 1785–1914. 113 containers, 11,290 items. Microfilm.

225
Hay papers. Hay, John, 1838–1905. Papers. 1 container, 1 item (roll of microfilm). Microfilm. (Original at Brown University, Providence, Rhode Island)

226
Mahan papers. Mahan, Alfred Thayer, 1840–1914. Naval officer and author. Papers, 1861–1913. 5 items.

Letters concerning U.S. defense policy and the Panama Canal. (2)

227
Monroe papers. Monroe, James, 1758–1831. Papers, 1758–1839. 76 containers, 5,000 items. Microfilm.

228
Moody papers. Moody, William Henry, 1853–1917. Papers, 1879–1916. 17 containers, 3,000 items.

Moody was Secretary of the Navy in 1903. This collection contains a few communications with the commander of the *Nashville* during the critical period in November of that year. (3)

229
Moore papers. Moore, John Bassett, 1860–1947.
Papers. Container 134.

230
Morgan papers. Morgan, John Tyler, 1824–
1907. Papers, 1857–1907. 36 containers, 9,000
items.

Senator Morgan of Alabama for many years
was the undisputed and unflagging leader in the
Senate of the fight for a Central American canal
under exclusive American control. He champi-
oned the Nicaragua route down to the last vote,
but after the Panama route prevailed, he continued to fight just as hard for undiluted American
control of the Panama Canal and Canal Zone.
(2)

231
Roosevelt papers. Roosevelt, Theodore, 1858–
1919. Papers, 1759–1920. 1,148 containers,
276,000 items. Microfilm.

232
Root papers. Root, Elihu, 1845–1937. Papers,
1863–1937. 262 containers, 66,000 items.

233
Spooner papers. Spooner, John Coit, 1843–
1919. Papers, 1855–1909. 203 containers, 10,000
items.

234
Taft papers. Taft, William Howard, 1857–1930.
Papers, 1810–1930. 2,801 containers, 675,000
items. Microfilm.

V. Sundry Nonlegal Periodicals

Because of the literally thousands of items extant under this heading, with more pouring out every day, the entries herein are agonizingly selective and cannot pretend to do much more than represent one person's opinion of some of the more interesting and significant highlights, and call attention to the existence of this vast store of material. The classic complaint of journalists that they are "writing on water" is, of course, quite true. Much fine writing in this genre uplifted inquiring minds for a day, then swiftly vanished beneath the wave of the next day's newspaper or the next issue of the magazine, seldom or never to be read again. At the least, the entries which follow are worth digging out to be read once again by anyone who is interested in the subjects of this bibliography. There are undoubtedly many other items of a periodical nature which have something of value to say, but which will have to be left to the determined researcher to discover through his own efforts.

235
Allan, Donald A. and Sherman, George. Panama: distrust and delay. The Reporter, v. 30, Feb. 27, 1964: 28–29.   D839.R385, v. 30

Written shortly after the riots of January 9–12, 1964, and before the resumption of diplomatic relations on April 3, 1964, this article is chiefly useful as a reminder that the riots had not come without ample warnings, which were unheeded, and as a detailed recapitulation of the difficulties encountered immediately afterward over the terms of renewing relations: "We had not negotiated peacefully when we had a chance; now we refused to negotiate 'under the gun.' "

In the light of hindsight, this work is overly optimistic about the future, assuming that a relatively easy solution would be to build a sea-level canal, under international control, while gradually turning the lock canal over to Panama. (2)

236
Baldwin, Hanson W. The Panama Canal—A sea-level project would change U.S. position in area. New York times, Aug. 12, 1960, p. L–5, and Aug. 13, 1960, p. L–16.

Appearing as a two-part "News Analysis" by a well-known journalist with credentials as a military expert, this entry is chiefly useful at the present time for capturing a picture of the overall problem, with emphasis on the military aspects, as it appeared in 1960. It helps a student of the subject to form an impression of how much things have changed and how much they have remained the same. One can see that serious consideration was being given to the idea of a sea-level canal through the Province of Darien as well as through other countries outside Panama. Mention is made of a State Department program envisioning a long-term plan, the original version of which included an eventual transfer of the present canal to Panama, but this provision, Baldwin implies, was withdrawn because of violent opposition from the Pentagon. (2)

237
A belated confession. New York times, Mar. 25, 1911, p. 10, column 3.

This is an editorial commenting on Theodore Roosevelt's famous (or infamous, depending on the point of view) speech of March 23, 1911, at Berkeley, California, in which he declared:

I am interested in the Panama Canal because I started it. If I had followed traditional, conservative methods I would have submitted a dignified State paper of probably 200 pages to Congress and the debates on it would have been going on yet; but I took the Canal Zone and let Congress debate; and while the debate goes on the canal does also.

This is one of the most often quoted statements in American political history: with approval by Roosevelt's admirers, and as a confession of guilt by his detractors. As may be inferred from the heading, the *Times* was not an admirer.

As reported by the *San Francisco Examiner,* what Roosevelt actually said was not "I took the Canal Zone," but "I took the isthmus." Whichever version is correct, the "taking" remains and that is what the *Times* was complaining about. (1)

238

An embassy from Colombia—Identity of party at Galveston now known—To ask that the recognition of Panama be rescinded. New York times, Nov. 19, 1903, p. 2.

Datelined Galveston, Texas, this story, immediately following the story about the signing of the Hay-Bunau Varilla Treaty (entry 261), reports the arrival in Galveston of a special embassy of three diplomats appointed by President Marroquín of Colombia who are on their way to Washington to "request the Washington Government to rescind its action in recognizing the Government of Panama, and who are also authorized to make a canal treaty with the United States at once on the latter's own terms." (2)

239

Geyelin, Philip. The irksome Panama wrangle. The Reporter, v. 30, Apr. 9, 1964: 14–17.

D839.R385, v. 30

This article is, in a sense, a sequel to entry 235, purporting to give details of the continuing wrangle over terms of renewing relations. On one level it is seen as a slightly ridiculous semantic dispute: Did the United States agree to "negotiate" (the Panamanian position) or to "discuss" (the United States position)? After two or three crises, President Johnson conceded that the dispute was "sticky" and "amiably substituted 'review,' which by some accounts was all that President Chiari wanted." On another level, however, a very touchy political issue was involved, as "those in this country who consider the 1903 canal pact inviolable" would have construed the word "negotiate" as a commitment in advance to revision of the treaty. (As we now know, such a commitment was avoided in the reestablishment of diplomatic relations, only to be made voluntarily a little later.) (2)

240

Gibbs, H. H. A southwest passage. *In* United States Naval Institute. Proceedings, v. 95, Apr. 1969: 64–73.   V1.U8, v. 95

Rear Adm. H. H. Gibbs, U.S. Navy (Retired), offers a startling and intriguing solution to the whole problem of sovereignty and the canal. He would build a "land canal" entirely across U.S. territory in the form of a super-railroad from Corpus Christi to San Diego capable of carrying huge bulk carloads at very high speed. The author, a graduate of the U.S. Naval Academy and a former associate professor of mechanical engineering, presents reasons why a land route is preferable to a sea-level canal. (2)

241

Handleman, Howard. What U.S. will yield in new deal for Panama. U.S. News & world report, v. 76, no. 7, Feb. 18, 1974: 64.

JK1.U65, v. 76

This article was written by a reporter who accompanied Secretary of State Kissinger to Panama City for the signing of the joint statement (entry 145) with Panama's foreign minister, Juan Antonio Tack, on February 7, 1974. It is objective and strictly factual, pointing out that the joint statement amounts to an agreement in principle to eventually turn over complete control of both the Canal Zone and the canal to Panama, but listing the several specific areas of disagreement which will have to be resolved before the principle can be implemented in the form of a new treaty. (2)

242

Harding, Earl. In justice to Colombia: how to settle the dispute which arose when we "took" Panama—the wide importance of the problem in South America—for a wider Canal Zone. World's work, v. 26, Oct. 1913: 675–680. map.

AP2.W8, v. 26

An "Editor's Note" introduces this extraordinary article:

The author of this article went to the Isthmus of Panama and to Bogotá in 1909 and 1910 to dig out the hidden history of the Panama secession. In this way he was brought in contact with the Colombian people more intimately perhaps than any foreigner could be who had not his special mission. The result of his two-years' study of the Panama question was presented to the Foreign Affairs Committee of the House of Representatives under the Rainey Resolution (entry 111) to investigate the "taking" of Panama.

Mr. Harding here reveals the deep indignation and sense of injustice among the Colombians at the way the Province of Panama had been taken away by the United States in 1903. For example:

The latest official map of Colombia (1912) shows the "Canal under construction," but no American Canal Zone and no Panama Republic. Colombian school children are taught that the "Department of Panama" is still legally a part of their country; that its seizure was in violation of a sacred treaty and that no son of Colombia should relax his antipathy toward the United States until that wrong shall have been righted.

Mr. Harding proposes, among other things, that nearly all of Panama east of the canal be given back to Colombia. (This article was written shortly before the negotiation of the Thomson-Urrutia Treaty, entry 154.)

In entry 34 (published in 1959), Harding takes a hard line against any concessions to Panama, but still insists (p. 149–50) that Colombia was mistreated in 1903 and "that fact unfortunately cost the United States the distrust and ill will of all Latin America." (2)

243
Hudson, Richard. Storm over the canal. The New York times magazine, May 16, 1976: 18–26.

The gist of this article is well summarized in the subtitle: "The military and economic importance of the Panama Canal may be fading. But it has become a passionate political issue: 'humiliation' versus 'colonialism.' "

Most of the material is basically familiar, but it is updated and the article contains several interesting and pointed quotations from the most active participants in the controversy. The total effect is a useful contribution to an understanding of current political realities. (1)

244
If U.S. gives up Panama Canal. U.S. News & world report, v. 80, no. 21, May 24, 1976: 27–29.

This unsigned article may be viewed as a follow-up to entry 241, and is valuable only to a reader who has no other source of information. It does emphasize that, although keeping the canal open is much more economically important to Panama than to the United States, the Panamanians might resort to violence against their own economic interests if their nationalist emotions are sufficiently aroused. An insert (p. 29) which purports to simplify the legal arguments over "sovereignty" and "perpetuity" is only helpful up to a certain point, after which it becomes confusing and misleading. (3)

245
Krock, Arthur. The Panama crisis—Dispute called a consequence of the paradox of U.S. foreign policy. New York times, Jan. 19, 1964, p. E–13, columns 1–2.

Krock attributes both the "bloody anti-American riots in the Canal Zone" of January 1964 and the embarrassment of the United States at having to use military force to protect its presence there to "the extravagant 'anti-colonial' position of the United States in world politics." That position, he says, has encouraged the formation of new nations long before they were capable of self-government, and has condoned military aggression in the name of "anti-colonialism." He cites several examples of U.S. attitudes elsewhere which are inconsistent with its policy in Panama and which could be construed as encouraging Panamanian self-assertion. He also deplores the fact that the U.S. mission to establish peace after the January 1964 riots accepted two official versions, one of which allowed the Panamanians to use the Spanish word for "negotiate," thus leading to further unnecessary complications (see entry 239). He concludes by quoting a comment on Panama by Congressman L. F. Sikes of Florida: "What is needed, he said 'is a little realism in dealing with irresponsible nations. Our practice of jumping to do the bidding of half-pint nations has about convinced the world we are the softest mark in history.' " (2)

246
Lawmakers in Panama demand scrapping of U.S. canal treaty. New York times, Nov. 18, 1961, p. L–9, columns 2–3.

This story reports that the Panamanian National Assembly had passed a unanimous resolution calling for the unilateral abrogation of existing treaties with the United States regarding the Panama Canal and the Canal Zone. The resolution disregarded the position taken before the assembly earlier in the month by Foreign Minister Galileo Solís who had merely called for further negotiations covering several aspirations not achieved by the 1955 treaty. (2)

247
McGrath, Marcos G. Ariel or Caliban? Foreign affairs, v. 52, Oct. 1973: 75–95.   D410.F6, v. 52

The author, the archbishop of Panama, takes his title, as he reveals (p. 81), from a book written in 1900 by a Uruguayan author, "Ariel and Caliban: the values of the spirit versus ambitious material expansion." It is an eloquent plea for social and economic justice, intellectually written in global terms but applying these values to specific situations: inside Panama, and between Panama and the United States. He draws a parallel between the paternalistic exploitation by propertied Panamanian townspeople of the landless campesinos (poor farmers), and the attitude of many individuals and institutions in the United States toward Latin America. As to the former he admits that: "the situations of injustice existing in Latin America, internally speaking, are our own fault. We cannot lay the blame on the United States or anyone else." But as to the latter, he cites facts and figures demonstrating "inbuilt colonial injustice":

Experts on inter-American relations know the facts. But the people of the United States do not . . . . Will the U.S.

people learn to look beyond their borders and accept as a duty and an honor their world responsibility?

He quotes at some length from the press statement on the Panama Canal issue which he gave on the occasion of the UN Security Council meeting held in Panama in March 1973 (see entry 129), in which he said: "The Church cannot stand aloof from these questions .... Morally the justice of the Panamian position regarding the Canal and the Canal Zone is unquestionable."

Archbishop McGrath was born in the Canal Zone and both his parents were U.S. citizens. In the 1940s, however, he renounced any claim to U.S. citizenship and opted for exclusive Panamanian citizenship. (2)

248
McLellan, A. G. The Panama Canal versus American shipping. North American review, v. 193, Jan. 1911: 111–120.   AP2.N7, v. 193

This article is selected as representative of many appearing about this time which speculated on the effect the opening of the canal would have on American merchant shipping, especially in the light of competition with foreign shipping which would also be using the canal. The author discusses advantages to American naval power which will accrue from fortification of the waterway (p. 120): "It would be lunacy on the part of America were she to leave unfortified what all military experts unite in regarding as the inevitable scene of the next war in the Western Hemisphere."

He argues that equal advantages to American merchant shipping are possible but will not result unless changes are made in American law and policy relative thereto (p. 114–15): "The remedy to prevent the decline or the total extinction of the American merchant marine is entirely in American hands .... The curse of America—the railroad trusts—will endeavor to frustrate all attempts ... to engage in long-distance coastal trading. ..." (3)

249
Mahan, Alfred Thayer. Fortify the Panama Canal. North American review, v. 193, Mar. 1911: 331–339.   AP2.N7, v. 193

The date of publication makes this article contemporaneous with a series of legal treatises previously cited (entries 198–203) on the subject. The renowned Admiral Mahan, looking at the question strictly as a matter of military and naval strategy, comes down squarely on the side of fortification. He recognizes that his view may seem inconsistent with his own well-known position as an advocate of the overriding role of sea power; but, in reply, quotes his own book (p. 332): "Navies do not dispense with fortifications

nor with armies; but, when wisely handled, they may save their country the strain which comes when these have to be called into play."

For the particular purposes of this bibliography, the most interesting point is that the military argument, which is quite logically presented, is weakened by dependence on an introductory premise which is highly questionable in law (p. 331):

In approaching the question of fortifying the Panama Canal, it is well to remember at once that the Canal Zone, with the qualified exceptions of the cities of Colon and Panama, is *United States territory* [italics added]. In the treaty of cession [there is no cession in the Hay-Bunau Varilla Treaty] .... It is also to be remembered that, besides being *American soil* [italics added] .... (2)

250
The Panama Canal record. v. 1–34, no. 9,: Sept. 4, 1907–Apr. 30, 1941. Panama Canal, Balboa Heights, Canal Zone, 1908–41. 34 v. illus.
                                                    TC774.A1P3

Weekly, 1907–June 1933; monthly, July 1933–1941.

V. 1–9 have title *Canal Record*.

Published under the authority and supervision of the Isthmian Canal Commission 1907–Mar. 1914; of the Panama Canal, April 1914–1941.

No more published.

Started by Colonel Goethals as a kind of morale booster, this publication was a way of keeping all the far-flung divisions of the enterprise informed of what was going on in the other divisions. It is invaluable as a primary source of Canal Zone history, not only because of the authentic tidbits of personal and local news but also because it printed current directories of officials, statistics, and organizational tables. The first issue contained the following "Announcement":

The primary purpose of *The Canal Record* is the publication of accurate information, based upon official records, concerning all branches of the work of Canal construction. So far as practicable, the progress made week by week, month by month, and year by year will be shown in comparable tables of statistics. In addition there will be published such information in regard to the social life of the Zone, its amusements, sports and other activities, as is thought to be of general interest. Space will also be given to letters from employees relating to any topic upon which they may choose to write, subject only to the restrictions that such communications must be couched in respectful language and must be signed in each instance with the name and address of the writer.

Joseph B. Bishop, who might be considered the quasi-official historian of the Isthmian Canal Commission (ICC), had this to say about it (entry 11): "It increased the efficiency of the force, welded it into a single body, and made it more contented. By giving space also to the social life and activities of the Canal Zone, this beneficial influence was augmented." In a sense, it might be thought of as complementary to the annual reports of the ICC in the same way that a small town weekly newspaper is complementary to the *New York Times*.

Despite its importance to Canal Zone history, it is placed in category 3 in this bibliography because it was distinctly inward looking, having little interest in international law or international relations. (3)

251

Panama Canal review. v. 1, May 1950 [Balboa Heights, Canal Zone] illus.   HE2830.P2P3

Frequency varies.

Official publication of the Panama Canal Company.

Supplements accompany some numbers.

This periodical might be considered a continuation of the *Panama Canal Record* (entry 250) which expired in 1941. Less inward looking, however, it contains many articles on the life and culture of Panama and seems to make a conscientious effort to help bridge the cultural gap between Zonians and Panamanians. Originally published only in English and at a frequency which varied, it is now published twice a year in both English and Spanish editions. (3)

252

The Panama dishonor. Nation, v. 77, Nov. 12, 1903: 374–375.   AP2.N2, v. 77

The *Nation* printed this article only a few days after the Panamanian revolt as an immediate reaction to the "sudden separation of the State of Panama from Colombia." It strongly condemns the precipitate recognition of Panama by the United States, asking rhetorically how this country would have reacted if Great Britain or France had recognized the Confederate States of America which had an infinitely more convincing claim to de facto independence than did the State of Panama on November 6, 1903. The article concludes: "There is a clear disregard of both law and morals in all this. Even the buccaneers who sailed the Spanish Main would have found it too much for them."

It does not necessarily follow, of course, that the *Nation* spoke for the nation. The first legal treatise on the subject (entry 193) appeared in December 1903 and thus it too was an almost immediate reaction. Given the normally slower pace of the law, it probably represented more accurately the ambivalence of feeling which Roosevelt's action provoked. (2)

253

Panama secedes from Colombia—Independence of Isthmus proclaimed—republic is declared. New York times, v. 53, Nov. 4, 1903, p. 1, columns 1–2.

History comes alive in this front page story. The first dispatch is datelined "Panama, Colombia, Nov. 3," but contains the information that "[Colombian] Gens. Tovar and Amaya, who arrived this morning, were imprisoned in the name of the Republic of Panama." The second dispatch, from Colón, mentions that a battalion of 450 well-armed soldiers under the command of General Tovar "arrived this morning . . . Gen. Tovar left for Panama [City] this morning, but the troops will remain here."

The third and longest part of the story is datelined "Washington, Nov. 3," and is headed "America to send warships." Perhaps the most noteworthy excerpts are:

There is a very general belief that the rejection of the Panama Canal treaty by Colombia caused the people of the Isthmus to decide to set up a government of their own, but none of the officials of the administration would authorize any statement to the effect that this was the case.

It is positively stated that these movements on the part of our navy are in no way connected with a canal project. . . .

The object of the revolutionary party is said to be an endeavor to bring about the annexation of the Isthmus of Panama to the United States and the subsequent completion of the Panama Canal under American auspices. (2)

254

Perpetual pacts declared invalid. New York times, Mar. 31, 1957, p. 15, columns 1–2.

This story reports on a "round-table discussion of the juridical aspects of the Panama and Suez Canals" sponsored by the University of Panama and attended by experts and professors of international law from Panama, Cuba, Costa Rica, Chile, Mexico, Guatemala, Nicaragua, and Honduras. The former Panamanian foreign minister, Octavio Fábrega, declared agreements in perpetuity should be considered invalid under international law as inconsistent with the sovereignty of the nation within which the canal lies. Dr. Francisco Alvarado García of the University of Havana took the position, however, that Panama could not, under international law, denounce her 1903 canal treaty with the United States. (2)

255

Roosevelt, Theodore. The Panama blackmail treaty. Metropolitan, v. 41, Feb. 1915: 8–10, 69–72.   AP2.M5, v. 41

The "blackmail treaty" which Roosevelt refers to in this article was the Thomson-Urrutia Treaty with Colombia (see entry 154) signed at Bogotá, April 6, 1914, but not proclaimed until March 30, 1922, because of the bitter opposition to it led by Roosevelt. He not only uses this article to attack the treaty, but as a vehicle for "explaining" the whole Panama affair and justifying his conduct therein. It is the most complete exposition in any one place of Roosevelt's version of the matter in his own words. The *Metropolitan* magazine is now defunct. (See also entry 257.) (1)

256
Rosenfeld, Stephen S. The Panama negotiations—a close-run thing. Foreign affairs, v. 54, Oct. 1975: 1–13.   D410.F6, v. 54

One of the most recent articles on the subject by an informed and reputable journalist (Rosenfeld writes frequently on foreign affairs for the *Washington Post*), this is a well-rounded and carefully researched treatment which touches on most of the major elements involved in the controversy. The situation is brought up to date as of October 1975. Recommended reading as a good summary of the current state of negotiations, an accurate and objective identification of the array of personalities and forces involved, and a realistic appraisal of the chances for a satisfactory outcome.

In sum, it is far from certain that all the pieces will eventually be put together, but this now seems possible, if not likely, to some of those closest to the process .... The Canal is an issue on which, one hopes, the right outcome is resulting in terms of the country's broad national interests. This is coming about, however, less from an orderly analysis and common perception of those interests than from an unchanneled process that reflects all of the diffusion of purposes and fragmentation of power current in Washington today. (p. 13) (1)

257
Stone, Melville E., Jr. Theodore Roosevelt—please answer. Metropolitan, v. 34, June 1911: 265–278. ports.   AP2.M5, v. 34

This article was written by the editor of the magazine himself as the lead for that issue. It severely attacks the way Roosevelt handled the "Panama affair," referring not only to Roosevelt's alleged violations of international law in his treatment of Colombia, but raising pointed questions about who received the $40 million supposedly paid to the (French) New Panama Canal Company. The article is prefaced by the following "Editor's Note":

The mere mention of the "Panama Scandal" is anathema to the average pro-Rooseveltian. . . . As a matter of fact the true story has never been told—it can never be told except by Mr. Roosevelt himself. The whole transaction has been surrounded with so much mystery that suspicion of evil-doing has naturally crept in and rumors of graft and corruption have come to be considered as being actual history. These stories could be silenced on the instant if Mr. Roosevelt would only come out in the open and answer what the people really want to know.

Roosevelt told his own story four years later in the same magazine (entry 255), but without referring to the Stone article and without answering the questions about the $40 million. (1)

258
Stratton, James H. Sea level canal: how and where. Foreign affairs, v. 43, Apr. 1965: 513–518.   D410.F6, v. 43

This article was written shortly after President Johnson's announcement of December 18, 1964 (entry 140) that the United States is prepared to negotiate a new basic canal treaty and proceed with plans for a sea-level canal. It speculates on the choice of routes and construction methods, conventional or nuclear. The author's solution is to convert the existing canal to sea level by conventional means, "and there can be no excuse for failure to achieve it." (3)

259
Thayer, William R. John Hay and the Panama Republic, from the unpublished letters of John Hay. Harper's Magazine, v. 131, July 1915: 165–175. ports.   AP2.H3, v. 131

In this commentary Hay's biographer probably reached a wider audience than did his book, *The Life and Letters of John Hay*. With respect to Hay's part in the birth of the Republic of Panama, however, the principal points made are the same as those set forth in the annotation to entry 67. (2).

260
Travis, Martin B. and Watkins, James T. Control of the Panama Canal: an obsolete shibboleth? Foreign affairs, v. 37, Apr. 1959: 407–418.   D410.F6, v. 37

The authors' answer to the question posed in the title is clearly foreshadowed in the first few lines:

Has American policy with respect to the Panama Canal outlived its usefulness? Changes in technology, in the international power structure and in the climate of world opinion would suggest that it has. In an age when the United States is turning increasingly to international arrangements to protect its interests on other continents, its position regarding the Canal becomes increasingly inconsistent, if not embarrassing. It might well embroil us in a struggle, initially one-sided, in which all Latin America would move to defend the sovereignty of a sister republic and the principles of self-determination and nonintervention.

They present facts and figures downplaying the importance of the canal to the United States as a physical object, and emphasizing its importance as a symbol. They introduce their solution with (p. 416): "A storm is building up in Panama. Appropriate measures taken soon can protect the real as distinguished from the illusory United States interests in the Canal, while a policy of drifting along may jeopardize our interests far beyond Central America." Words to which it is rather difficult to take exception. The solution itself—to internationalize the canal under an instrumentality of the United Nations—appears to be on less solid ground. (2)

261
Treaty for canal made with Panama—Sovereignty over territory for United States—The convention signed. New York times, Nov. 19, 1903, p. 1–2.

This story reports the signing of the Hay-Bunau Varilla Treaty the previous evening "in Secretary Hay's study." Perhaps the most interesting excerpt is the following paragraph:

The keynote of the treaty is the provision in one of the very first articles, by which Panama cedes to the United States whatever land or lands throughout the Republic of Panama this Government shall find desirable in connection with the building or the operation and maintenance of the canal. In addition the treaty gives to the United States absolute sovereignty over the canal strip, which, it is understood, comprises between eight and ten miles on each side of the canal [actually it comprises five miles on each side]. Within this zone the power of the United States is as absolute as if the zone were part and parcel of this country. (2)

Appendix
Miscellaneous Material Outside of the Library of Congress

Aside from the materials cited herein, there are a number of other less important collections outside of the Library of Congress, in the National Archives and elsewhere, which time and space do not permit listing and which, in any case, would not be likely to make any substantial additional contribution, except for some highly specialized purpose.

262

Herran papers. Archives, Georgetown University, Washington, D.C. 5 containers, 97 folders, 3 letter books.

This collection contains the incoming and outgoing papers—e.g., letters, cables, notes, and clippings—of the Colombian legation in Washington from 1898 to 1904. Thus, it covers the negotiations leading up to the signing of the Hay-Herrán Treaty, the rejection of that treaty, the Panamanian Revolution, and the signing of the Hay-Bunau Varilla Treaty. Tomás Herrán, the compiler, was chargé d'affaires when he took over the legation on November 28, 1902, upon the abrupt departure of the previous envoy, José Vicente Concha. Mr. Herrán was a graduate of Georgetown University. (2)

263

International rights of passage under a new Panama Canal Treaty. Report of American Bar Association, Subcommittee on International Waterways.

This is an unpublished document distributed in June 1975. The committee takes no position on whether existing treaty arrangements should be changed, maintaining this to be a political question beyond the scope of the report, but proceeds on the assumption that a new treaty will be drafted in accordance with the eight principles of the Kissinger-Tack joint statement of February 7, 1974 (see entry 145).

The committee addresses itself to the issue of international rights of passage because it believes that such rights are not adequately safeguarded at present. This is so as only three states (the United States, Panama, and the United King-dom) are parties to the Hay-Pauncefote and the Hay-Bunau Varilla treaties, and there is no publicly available evidence that international rights of passage are being considered in current treaty negotiations. Thus, the committee seems to take a different view from that favored by Edwin C. Hoyt (entry 37) in 1966. In the last paragraph (p. 309) Hoyt suggests that an international right of passage, based on custom and prescription, would extend even to nonsignatories of the original treaties, adding that a simple declaration by the United States or the insertion in the treaty with the territorial sovereign of a declaration respecting the general right of free passage would be sufficient.

The report concludes by recommending that whenever operation of the canal is relinquished to Panama, treaty obligations should become effective mandating that:

1. The Republic of Panama perpetually maintain the Canal in good repair;
2. All applicable tolls and regulations be applied on a nondiscriminatory basis;
3. Tolls be "reasonable" or (preferably) subject to a ceiling specified in a formula set forth in the treaty; and
4. Regulations applicable to peacetime operations and any additional regulations applicable in wartime be "reasonable" or (preferably) subject to specific standards set forth in the treaty.

The report also recommends that: (a) disputes be irrevocably submitted to the International Court of Justice or, preferably, to binding arbitration; (b) the Republic of Panama be made permanently neutral; and (c) Panama's neutrality and contractual obligations with third party states be made specific by reciprocal agreements with such states. (1)

264
Records of the Panama Canal, Washington National Records Center, Archives Branch, Record Group No. 185.

Some guidance to these materials is available in a compilation by Richard W. Giroux and Garry D. Ryan entitled *Preliminary Inventory of Textual Records of the Panama Canal (Record Group 185)* (Washington, National Archives, National Archives and Records Service, General Services Administration, 1963. 36 p. U.S. National Archives. Publication no. 63–20. Preliminary inventories, no. 153. CD3026.A32, no. 153).

Covering the time span 1881–1938, this collection is a priceless treasure trove of primary (and sometimes extremely raw) material. The only serious criticism that could be made of it has already been expressed in the foreward to the above-cited publication 63–20:

These inventories are called "preliminary" because they are provisional in character. They are prepared as soon as possible after the records are received without waiting to screen out all disposable material or to perfect the arrangement of the records.

Hence, the researcher must be patient as there is a fair amount of duplication; sought-after topics may be found in unexpected and seemingly illogical places. For purposes of this bibliography the most pertinent entries are: (79) Foreign Affairs, (80) Panama Republic, and (94) Law and Government. (1)

265
Special Panama Collection of the Canal Zone Library-Museum. 10,000 items, many unique.

The strongest part of the collection covers the planning and construction of the canal. Also included are such varied materials and topics as exploration and early voyages (with early editions of Dampier, Ulloa, and Exquemelín, and reprints of Hakluyt), treaty matters, and periodical articles.

The holdings of this special collection (as of early 1964) are listed in the *Subject Catalog of the Special Panama Collection of the Canal Zone Library-Museum; the History of the Isthmus of Panama as It Applies to Interoceanic Transportation* (Boston, G. K. Hall, 1964. x1, 341 p. Z1500.C35). (1)